TH GRIND CULTURE DETOX

THE GRIND CULTURE DETOX

Heal Yourself from the Poisonous
Intersection of Racism, Capitalism,
and the Need to Produce

HEATHER ARCHER

Hierophantpublishing

Cover design by Laura Beers
Cover art by ©shutterstock/svekloid
Print book interior design by Frame25 Productions

Hierophant Publishing
San Antonio, TX
www.hierophantpublishing.com

If you are unable to order this book from your local bookseller,
you may order directly from the publisher.

Library of Congress Control Number: 2022932446
ISBN: 978-1-950253-25-8

10 9 8 7 6 5 4 3 2 1

For my ancestors who have paved the way for a conversation long overdue. Your care and wisdom illuminated my path when it was hard to see the light.

And for Cole. Thank you for showing me that another way is possible.

Why is everything so rushed?
When did quick become the standard of desires?
Why is fast paced given authority
over a slow and steady flow?
It's time to detox from grind culture.
It's time to rest.

—Tricia Hersey, creator of the Nap Ministry

Contents

Introduction

When it comes to work, something's not working in America.

The average American works more hours than workers in any other country in the world. Although most industrialized nations have laws that limit the hours of a workweek, the United States has yet to be included on this list. According to a recent Gallup poll, the average workweek for full-time employees in the United States is forty-seven hours—that's almost an extra full day of work every week. Although many economists in the past predicted that our current time period would be an age of leisure, this is far from being our reality.

Out of almost 200 countries, 134 have laws that cap the maximum number of hours an employee can work. The United States is the only industrialized nation without laws setting a maximum number of hours that you can legally work in a week. The United States is also the only industrialized country in the world without national paid parental leave, as well as the only industrialized nation without a federal law that mandates paid sick leave for employees.

Since 1950, we have seen the average number of hours Americans work in a day continue to climb, despite numerous studies that show that productivity diminishes after logging in longer hours. In a 2004 report from the CDC called "Overtime and Extended Work Shifts," a number of studies showed that "the 9th to 12th hours of work were associated with feelings of decreased alertness and increased fatigue, lower cognitive function, declines in vigilance on task measures, and increased injuries." The question has to be asked: *What exactly are we working for?*

The answer is grind culture.

Grind culture is a phrase that points to the confluence of societal beliefs, expectations, and practices whose simple message is this: In order to be considered valuable or worthy in our society, one must be economically productive.

It's an insidious and ubiquitous idea. And it's ruining our lives.

Grind culture impacts anyone and everyone, regardless of gender, race, or social class. However, if you are a person of color, female, disabled, or in almost any other minority group, it can impact you on a deeper level particularly. Because these groups are not politically dominant, they already receive messages from the culture at large that they are less valuable, and because of this they often try to produce *more* just to be seen or accepted in grind culture society.

Many of us understand the misery and dehumanization that grind culture inflicts, yet we find ourselves perpetuating the same cycles of harm and continued participation because we don't believe that another way is possible. Most of us know we're overworked. Many of us have firsthand knowledge of this harmful side of capitalism and the way it has created large-scale dehumanization, waste, and exploitation, but most people resign themselves to the idea that this is "just the way things are." If you push people on the issue, some will roll their eyes and write you off as a crunchy hippie socialist who has their head in the clouds. Others will ask how they can possibly make ends meet if not through the unrelenting crush of the daily grind. We are all locked in a castle of toxic productivity, and the dragon feels too large to slay.

But I refuse to believe grind culture is an unstoppable force. While there is no denying that it permeates all aspects of our culture, its strength ultimately lies in our acceptance and participation. *We* give it power, and therefore *we can withdraw that power.* In ways both great and small we have the ability to intervene and achieve liberation from grind culture. It might be awkward, confusing, and even painful at first as we struggle to create new habits and boundaries, but I assure you, it can be done.

You possess unconditional worthiness, and throughout this journey I will be reminding you of that. There is an innate divine power within you that is not made better or diminished in any way by whether you produce or not. This power is inherent in you; no one can give it to you, and no one can take it away. You are a sacred and sovereign being. These pages are filled with practical tools to help you activate that power so that you may live a life rooted in prosperity and liberation.

I wrote this book to shed light on grind culture—to name it, unearth it, and reclaim our power from it. I wrote this book in response to a myriad of questions I've received from students and clients about how to authentically incorporate well-being into their daily lives and to reinvent their relationship with work.

Which brings me to an important lesson right away: *Grind culture is not the same as work.* It can be hard to believe this, since so many of us have never been taught or experienced another way of working. For now, I want you to know that it is more than possible to embrace work, to tap into productivity when you want to, to pursue passion projects, to follow your dreams and sense of purpose, and much more—all while rejecting the influence of grind culture.

My Story

A few years ago I was the director of a residential summer camp in the San Francisco Bay Area. This camp was a healing-centered program for African American youth to unpack racial and intergenerational trauma in order to experience collective healing and self-actualization. With a thirty-year history in the community, many staff members had definitive childhood experiences at this camp in their own youth. Many young people, families, and community members had a special stake in this program because of its long lineage of healing and transformation.

During the week of camp, we served seventy-five youth who learned about African history and unpacked gender-based violence and cultivated healing circles of cisgender, queer, and gender nonbinary youth. Camp youth soaked in practices such as yoga and sound healing experiences to promote healing and well-being.

On paper, we were doing all the right things to culti-vate a healing space. In reality though, as a collective, we were stressed, overworked, and sleep-deprived. Although the camp focused on healing and well-being for its par-ticipants, the preparation and completion of the experience proved spiritually draining, overwhelming, and even trau-matic for the adults involved.

As the leader of this experience, I perpetuated this environment of overwork and overwhelm. I read and responded to emails at all hours, accepted late-night phone calls, and neglected my own work-life boundaries while caring for my six-month-old son, Cole. I had little grace for myself and even felt guilty for taking breaks to pump breast milk or stopping the workday in order to pivot and care for my son.

Despite the intensely emotional nature of this camp experience, we scheduled it in such a way that left little room for breaks or moments of pause and reflection. Though this experience afforded meaningful moments for youth and staff to unpack important issues like race and gender, it also caused harm. To fulfill our mission, I believed, we had to sacrifice rest, ease, and taking things slowly. In my mind, it just wasn't possible to do both.

The camp was rife with contradictions. Although many of the youth reported to their parents that they had an amazing and transformational experience, I left that camp feeling like I had failed as a leader and organizer. I was unable to personally integrate the healing and well-being that we preached to our participants. In addition, I felt like a fraud. I was supposed to embody and model healing and wellness but couldn't even set and hold firm boundaries to advocate for myself and my family. I felt defeated.

On the second to last day of camp, I broke down. I had gone sixteen hours without eating, and I was working over fourteen hours a day while breastfeeding. Time and time again throughout the planning experience, I chose work over my own needs and the needs of my family, and where did it get me? I was on the verge of a dangerous meltdown. While I had been in toxic work environments before, something changed in me that summer. I finally understood at the deepest level that my ideas and habits about work were faulty. I hadn't lost my passion for doing something so essential for the community, but *I had to find another way to work.*

To begin to uncover a new way forward, I had to contend with something I'd felt in my bones for a long time but had never been able to articulate until that summer. I'd seen its effects in generations of my own family. I'd watched its ebbs and flows in the cities and communities in which I lived, in the schools and workplaces I moved through. As a new mother passionate about my work and career, I had been nearly undone by it. This dragon I had to slay was grind culture.

That started me on a journey to learn all I could about the origin of grind culture and all the ways it manifests in our society—and, most importantly, how I could change it. For my part, I am still unlearning the harmful belief systems imposed by society that assert that success means putting work above all else. I spent many years pouring energy, time, and hard-won knowledge into my job at the expense of my health, family, and well-being. I ran an endless marathon on a hamster wheel of scarcity, and then wondered what was wrong with me when I felt drained and depleted.

In order to shift this narrative, I had to step back, rest, reflect, and realign with my values. I had gone so far down the path of grind culture that I didn't even know what my personal thriving would look or feel like. As I began to cultivate practices and rituals to transform my relationship with productivity, I moved from surviving to thriving in my work and personal life. As I began to lead others through this journey, my eyes opened even further to the profound need for this work and the rewards of this process of disentangling ourselves from grind culture.

Initiating Your Grind Culture Detox Journey

Where does this journey start?

It starts with *awareness*.

As in most things, we cannot begin to do better—to move forward with ourselves and our lives—until we know where we are right now. Often, we're not even conscious about how we are inflicting grind culture onto ourselves, our coworkers, our employees, and our family members. Of course, the bigger picture is critically important too, and in this book we'll explore the history of grind culture and many of its present manifestations as well as how it intersects with racism, classism, sexism, and ableism. But we won't be able to get anywhere on a personal, local, and daily level without building *self*-awareness.

Embarking on the journey of detoxing from grind culture requires more than an intellectual knowing of what grind culture is and how it currently impacts us. So in addition to understanding the complexities of grind culture on a global and historical scale, we also must ask ourselves about our own beliefs about work, balance, wellness, and our value as human beings. How do those beliefs show up in our actions? How might we want to change on a personal level, and how might we effect change in our communities and society as a whole? We all possess a deeper knowing in our bodies, in our ancestral traditions (whatever they may be), and in our universal capacity to dream the future into being. Our detox journey will call on our whole selves and will benefit from a wide variety of modalities.

I want to also address the idea of toxicity and why I use the term *detox* when I talk about our journey toward recognizing and healing ourselves of grind culture. The truth is that in some ways grind culture is like an addictive behavior. When you think of being addicted to a substance, like a harmful drug, most of us understand that often the first step to healing is to engage in a process of detoxification. During this time, addictive toxins leave your body, although it doesn't happen overnight. The process can feel painful and tedious.

However, we can't totally give up certain substances (like food) or behaviors (like working), even when they become addictive. So how can we detox when we can't give something up completely? I approach my work in my workshops as well as with my clients from a harm reduction framework. This is the answer to those who might argue that they can't stop grinding because they have to put food on the table and pay bills. They're of course correct about that in part—we do have to participate in the system as it is presently in order to survive—but we can do so in a way that also allows us to thrive, to be healthy, strong, and rested. We're not giving up work, but rather reimagining our relationship with it in a new and healthy way. The harm reduction model reminds us that there are practices we can return to and habits we can build that reclaim our right to thrive within our workday. If we get lost, we can always find our way back to center. Remember, this is about progress and not perfection.

By the end of this book, we'll have drilled down deeply together on the most essential questions that I encounter in my practice and teaching:

1. What is grind culture and how does it show up in my work and personal life?

2. What real-time tools and strategies can I implement to detox from grind culture and reclaim my time?

3. How can I unlearn grind culture to infuse ease and flow into my workday while still being productive?

4. What does it mean to access places of joy within my work schedule?

The first part of this book outlines the past and present of grind culture how we got here and how it shows up for us today. With this knowledge, we can unpack our own personal relationship to grind culture, and gain awareness into how we can radically reorient our relationship to the exhaustion, guilt, and dis-ease we feel as a result of grind culture.

The second part of the book explores specific ways we can detox from grind culture. We will explore the science and history of sleep and rest in ancient civilizations versus our current society and learn how to use rest to tap into our sacred, sovereign power. Next, we will focus on practices like somatics and sound that can provide powerful gateways to healing and growth. We will learn how grind culture is expressed in our personal and work relationships and how boundary-setting rituals and techniques can assist during detox. Next, we'll explore how to build and maintain spaces and practices that honor connection to nature and strengthen our sacred workspace.

Each chapter will include stories—some historical, some personal, and some shared by former clients and colleagues. At the end of the chapters, you'll find an affirmation and a series of questions or writing prompts and/or an activity or assignment that will deepen your understanding of the concepts and healing potentials in that chapter.

I encourage you to select and dedicate a journal specifically for this work, and if you'd like, you might also want to gather spiritual or healing objects whose energy and power can support you on this journey.

I also encourage you to take what is useful to you from this book and leave the rest. You don't have to do everything right now. Be gentle with yourself, and begin with those activities and exercises that resonate with you the most. I have found that when you begin the process of detoxing from grind culture, you will naturally gravitate toward more and more ways to put these ideas into practice, whether it's increasing your self-care, holding a boundary, or resetting your priorities. So be open to information, circumstances, and interactions that conspire to offer you lessons or challenges that can accelerate your growth and healing in surprising ways, but also recognize that this takes time and you don't have to do everything at once.

The good news is that when we make the decision to begin the process, healing becomes irresistible. Any difficulties we may face are soon dwarfed by the rewards of the healing itself. Furthermore, our personal healing ricochets out into the community and creates a ripple effect of collective healing.

Our North Star on this healing journey will be the reclaiming of our sovereignty. A world outside of grinding looks like releasing attachments to belief systems, people, and professions that don't recognize our inherent value as humans. A world outside of grind culture looks like an abundance of time to embody joy while cocreating a thriving society that honors our humanity. A world outside of grinding looks like taking the time and space to address our shadows and set healthy boundaries.

Joy is our birthright. Everyone deserves the ability to fully express themselves by sharing their natural gifts with the world, honoring their basic needs, and make a living wage. This is work-life liberation, or a way of working that honors the full spectrum of our humanity. Each one of us, regardless of age, ethnicity, or income, deserves room to explore, freedom to make mistakes, as well as ample time for mindful living, health, and well-being.

Holding a vision of healing for a world in pain is a courageous act. We are ushering in a new way of being, and as in labor, the pain and fear of the unknown can be intense. Breathe and push through. More is required of you. Stop waiting for permission to know you are worthy of your vision being fulfilled. You are worthy now.

Chapter 1

Grind Culture Explained

> After centuries of technological advances, why do we find
> ourselves working just as much as ever? Why do most people
> on earth still live in a daily experience of scarcity? For centu-
> ries, futurists have predicted an imminent age of leisure. Why
> has it never happened? The reason is that, at every oppor-
> tunity, we have chosen to produce more rather than to work
> less. We have been helpless to choose otherwise.
> —Charles Eisenstein, *Sacred Economics*

In 2009, palliative caregiver Bronnie Ware wrote an article called "Regrets of the Dying," where she explored her experiences caring for those at the end of their lives. The second regret from the top of the list, right behind wishing to live an authentic life, was, "I wish I hadn't worked so hard."

When we think back over the years we've spent on earth, I'm certain many of us will wish that we hadn't worked so hard. And yet, as Charles Eisenstein points out above, despite our advancements in technology, life expectancy, and general quality of life, we haven't stopped working so hard. In fact, we're working harder than ever. We can't take a break; we can't take time off; we are restless and unhappy when we are still; we can't sit in silence for more than five minutes. We feel guilty, exhausted, overwrought, yet helpless to change it.

This is grind culture.

Grind culture refers to our collective agreement that in order to be considered a valuable human being, one must be economically productive. Grind culture trains us to believe that if we're not producing, then we're not worthy. This is the shadow side of capitalism, which creates a society conditioned to equate success with production and orders the importance of people based on how much they produce. Everything else—family, friendships, happiness, leisure, rest—becomes secondary by our actions. In other words, we may say that work is not a higher priority than these, but our actions show otherwise. Grind culture is insidious and vast; it is baked into so many different systems and ways of being in our culture that it's hard to even see it sometimes.

On a personal level, you have most certainly experienced some or all of the symptoms of grind culture:

- A fear of stillness

- Feeling guilty about resting

- Viewing exhaustion as productive

- Sacrificing the needs of your body to produce

○ Overpacking your calendar

○ Never feeling satisfied with what you have

○ Thinking something is wrong with you when you are not productive

○ Competing with others over who grinds the hardest

○ Treating some people as though they are "more important" than others based on their profession

In fact, many of these symptoms are so common that they feel like our normal, everyday experience, but throughout this book we will examine how these personal symptoms correlate to systemic consequences. For instance, our fear of stillness and lack of satisfaction feed our addiction to social media, screens, and overconsumption of everything from alcohol to endless news cycles. Our guilt about resting and exhaustion lead to dangerous health consequences, from chronic diseases to car accidents. When we compete with others for status and resources, or when we deem some humans more important than others based on their job function (i.e., what they produce), we shut down our ability to cooperate, build community, and even find political and social common ground. In these ways and more, grind culture has negatively impacted our bodies, our minds, and the way we relate with one another.

Grind culture also objectifies Mother Earth and the plants, animals, and natural resources that are so vital to our own continued presence here. The environmental disasters we are currently facing are in large part the result of our grind culture, as we have put economic growth and productivity over the health and well-being of the planet. This devastation follows logically from grind culture thinking, because if we can't see ourselves as valuable without productivity, how can we see the true worth in a marsh, a mountain, or a flock of birds?

Deep down, we all know this assessment of our worth is ludicrous. We are sacred beings, born sovereign, whole and complete. The simple fact that we exist is miraculous. The way the universe bring us onto this human plane is remarkable. Consider that during conception, millions of sperm are exposed to an egg, yet only one will be able to complete conception. You are literally one in a million. When you are born, you come into this world with a set of unique gifts that only you can express. Grind culture has trained us to forget our own inherent worthiness and trade it in for a standard that is contingent upon our production.

Not only are we sacred, but we also live on sacred land. The earth orchestrates itself to provide nourishment and sustenance to all living beings that reside on this planet. Native cultures from around the world taught that the earth is itself a living organism, interconnected and alive. Every plant that exists on this planet has some kind of healing capacity, and yet even plants are valued and devalued in our grind culture based on their usefulness to production. When we set aside the fear and scarcity that lead to grind culture, we see that the truth of the matter is that we are held and cared for by the earth.

As a result of grind culture mentality, most of the sacred beings on this beautifully abundant planet are under the spell of materialism, manipulation, control, and coercion. This unfortunate dynamic helps construct things such as racism, gender-based oppression, and ableism. Grind culture provides the fuel to keep these toxic systems running.

The Myth of Scarcity

One of grind culture's tools in perpetuating its grueling machine is the myth of scarcity. In contemporary society, we are inundated with messages that there is "not enough" of the things we think we need. Because of this, so many of us are taught to see life as a competition, and we need to work hard to make sure we get our fair share.

While this scarcity message starts with the basic necessities like food, water, and shelter, it quickly moves on to coveted material possessions such as fancy cars, big homes, designer handbags, and the like.

But the myth of scarcity doesn't stop there, as it inevitably gets extended to nonmaterial things too, such as love, friendship, and happiness. Societal messaging tells us that these too are in short supply. Finally, we are told that we ourselves aren't enough, and therefore our main tasks in life involve striving to prove ourselves worthy and grinding tooth and nail to acquire our needs and achieve our goals before someone else does.

But is any of that true? Of course not.

First, there is more than enough of the basic necessities for everyone. The planet is an abundant giver of what is needed to sustain us, care for us, and see to our basic needs, and that includes food, water, and shelter. It's our relentless pursuit of more than enough—out into grotesque levels of acquisition, wealth, and power—that has kept us from prioritizing providing basic necessities for everyone, which is completely within our power to do right now.

Likewise, and possibly even more profoundly for us as individuals, there is an abundant supply of love, worth, happiness, rest, satisfaction, fulfillment, etc., for everyone. Whenever we receive messages telling us otherwise, we know that is the voice of grind culture trying to assert control.

The Productivity Trap

Another tricky way that grind culture operates is by convincing us that we are doing something "good" even as we harm ourselves, others, and the planet. A great example of this is our understanding of productivity.

Society tells us that working for long hours without breaks boosts productivity, and the dominant narrative in the working world is that we must maximize production in every moment of our day. Endless books and systems and programs are marketed to harried workers who think there must be a magic way to accomplish more. We are taught to work "against the clock" and are applauded for sacrificing breaks, meals, and family time to get more work accomplished. The carrot on the end of the stick is the idea that all our productivity will earn us rest. Yet time and space for that rest never seem to materialize.

Grind culture tricks us into believing that it's noble to work from a place of overwhelm, spend long hours staring at the computer screen, and stay late at night and come in on weekends to boost our productivity. Grind culture fails to mention that these practices actually lead to deteriorating states of health and well-being. Working nonstop throughout the day creates stress, which can lead to lower energy and burnout in the long run. Excessive amounts of time sitting and staring at screens can take years off our lives.

Any institution operating under the system of grind culture will be rooted in inequity and oppression. Grind culture would prefer not to see humanity from a nuanced spectrum of diversity and expansive identities, but rather as units of consciousness that can provide cheap labor to keep capitalism churning. With diverse identities comes complexity: more categories to create, more opinions to listen to, less time for production.

Grind Culture's Impact on Marginalized People

Grind culture impacts anyone and everyone, regardless of your gender, race, or social class. However, it can impact you on a deeper level if you are a person of color, female, or disabled. Since we live in a capitalist society that is structured on racial and gender hierarchy, people who are not part of the politically dominant gender or race are made to feel less valuable in overt and covert ways that go beyond grinding. We get this messaging in our schooling, our job market, and our everyday interactions. Because we get these messages of not being enough, we try to produce more to be seen and valued in this society. On the flip side, if you are a person with disabilities, you can find yourself shut out of the capitalist system and seen as a liability and an obstruction to the flow of production.

Seeing grind culture through this wide-angle lens is essential because it opens up the many facets and functions of the harm it causes. It also reminds us of our sacred selves and challenges us to support our fellow beings in communities of connection and care. No matter how hard we work and grind, we are all equal, made out of the same flesh and bones, and these encapsulating our sacred divinity. Any box this society attempts to put us in using productivity as a metric will create a lesser, flatter picture of the masterpiece that each and every one of us is.

Many of us have been duped into believing that working harder makes us smarter, which is simply not true. If anything, we're losing our brain capacity as a collective with the increase of distractions from our attention economy, as well as less space for rest and reflection within the workweek. Continuous productivity keeps us in a system of grinding and moves us further away from thriving in our personal and professional lives. We need to remain vigilant to interrupt this programming and see and believe that another way of living and working isn't only possible, but also on the way.

A healthy commitment to productivity begins with understanding that your value is not defined by what you do and produce. Your value is inherent and equal among all human beings; it cannot be built up or taken away.

When we really believe this, we can be productive in ways that don't rely on or reinforce grind culture. If our job requires us to sit much of the day, we can commit to physical activity, including regularly stretching or even standing up, both of which greatly increase blood circulation and promote the flow of oxygen. We can reevaluate stressful deadlines, a demanding workload, and endless projects or meetings, which prevent us from concentrating on tasks at hand and making intelligent decisions. We can remember for ourselves and reinforce for our colleagues that true, healthy productivity requires sleep and rest, good nutrition, physical health, human connection, and downtime to dream, play, and create outside of work. It's time to rewrite the rules regarding productivity to accommodate the basic functioning of the human brain and body.

Many of us have received the message to grind at all costs from our employers, who can be insensitive to our human needs. Left unchecked, over time we begin to treat our own bodies, minds, and spirits with a lack of self-regard in the name of keeping up with the system of grind culture. Although this notion of toxic productivity has been a part of the programming we've received throughout our lives, the time has come to hold space for the idea that another way of living and working is needed for us to thrive in the years to come.

Grind Culture and Perfectionism

Perfectionism is a form of self-harm rooted in the need to appear perfect or attain perfection as a threshold for self-worth and value in society. Perfectionism dims our resilience, eats up time and energy, blocks our courage, and thwarts the mistakes we have to be able to make in order to learn and grow. Much like grind culture itself, it confines us to a hamster wheel of "never enough" where we run ourselves into exhaustion, avoiding the needs of our bodies and the calls of our spirit.

A study by Thomas Curran and Andrew P. Hill examined how perfectionism has increased among college students in the United States, Canada, and the UK from 1989 to 2016 and suggested that large structural forces such as corporate influence in the media and politics have led to increased exposure to advertising and social media comparisons. The aphorism "comparison is the thief of joy" describes perfectionism's reliance on our natural human tendency to judge and evaluate ourselves and others.

Perfectionism thrives in exposure to unattainable standards. In the United States, white supremacy, patriarchy, sexism, and ableism define and uphold these standards. Rich, thin, white, cis male, straight, nondisabled bodies are held up as the most valued, everywhere from corporate hierarchies to mass marketing, educational, and political contexts. This leaves the vast majority of the world population undervalued for any number of reasons, vulnerable to the belief that attaining perfection is a worthy goal that might elevate a person's standing or ease their path. Even if we know this is not logically true, the feeling persists.

Perfectionism chips away at our humanity. We turn ourselves into objects, our time and lives into commodities that can be tweaked, improved, and traded in the name of profit, status, and worth. We cannot unpack the system of grind culture without examining the impact that perfectionism has had on our ways of feeling through and knowing the world.

Perfectionism manifests in the subliminal and overt messaging that we receive from advertisements, schooling, and cultural conditioning from an early age. These messages shape our overall self-worth and the value that we place on ourselves in society. Black liberation educator, author, and podcast host Monique Melton underlines the insidious nature of this messaging when she says, "I don't remember a distinct defining moment of 'Oh yeah, I am struggling with perfectionism' because it was never something that was framed as dehumanizing. It was just a part of my life, and it's been socialized as, 'this is the standard by which you measure your life.'"

When we convince ourselves or others that human beings are less or more valuable based on our physical, mental, or cultural attributes, or by how much we produce, we become susceptible to divisiveness, to systems of subjugation and control, and to war with each other as well as within ourselves. In the most extreme cases, this belief in supremacy and inferiority fuels human atrocities such as genocide and ethnic cleansing of those perceived to be of genetic or cultural inferiority or being less able to produce or contribute.

The spirit of perfectionism can seep past the self and mold societal norms and perceptions to the detriment of marginalized groups. Perfectionism hits differently when it's impacted by intersecting forms of oppression. For example, in a society that still upholds European features as the standard of beauty, people of color (or POC) are more impacted by the toxic ideology of body perfectionism than their white counterparts. Within grind culture, the people who hold the most political and economic power will determine what is successful and attractive and what is not, while people from marginalized communities and identities will be left striving and falling short of this unattainable ideal. This constant striving leads to serious emotional and spiritual harm.

Giving Ourselves Space

At this point, you likely have an idea of what grind culture is and how pervasive it can be in our society. In this way, grind culture, like the prescription for perfectionism it encompasses, can feel completely overwhelming when confronted for the first time. It's difficult to know where to begin. But I want to assure you that there is a way out from under the demands of grind culture, and one of the very first steps lies in allowing the process to unfold as gently as you need it to be. As Monique Melton puts it so powerfully, ". . . Give yourself space to feel your feelings for as long as you need to. Keep giving yourself permission to process your feelings without shame and without judgment. We can't blame ourselves for the internalized oppression when it's all around us. And so instead of blaming ourselves, we just can push some of that energy towards dismantling these oppressive structures."

It is in this spirit that we will move forward in this book, beginning with a pause to reflect on the impact of grind culture in our own personal lives before diving into some historical context. As we do so, I encourage you to remember Melton's words, and to *give yourself space*.

A Pause As We Begin

Reclaiming the Spirit of the Turtle

This land known as the United States did not always operate at such a fast-paced frenzy. Before conquest by European colonizers, North America was known by some Indigenous stewards of the land as Turtle Island. The name came from a variety of oral stories passed down, many of which include a turtle having the world on its back. In the story, the turtle represents the earth and the seat of creation. The turtle is a symbol for cultural identity, sovereignty, and reverence for the environment. It is well known for a slow, peaceful, steady pace, and the message it brings is to live in the moment, take time for pause and reflection, and enjoy the delights that life has to offer.

In 2020, the COVID-19 pandemic gave most of us a forced pause. Our vulnerability to this virus forced us to do what we haven't seemed able to do for a century or more: we had to slow down. Although frontline workers did not have the option to pause, notably in the health, food, and transportation industries, a large majority of people stayed home. Public spaces, schools, and businesses emptied out.

In this sacred pause, amid the heaviness of illness and loss, we realized the many ways that our compulsion to produce at all costs had taken a spiritual and physical toll. Additionally, scientists began noting our planet's positive response to our slowing down, as pollution was down in cities all over the world, including Paris, Bangalore, Boston, and Washington, DC. There were more sightings of wild animals. Pumas and coyotes were more noticeable, and sea turtles were seen boldly resting on beaches, nesting their eggs free from overpopulated shores and light pollution.

Meanwhile, parks and hiking trails were overcrowded with bored humans who could now take time to satisfy their urges to get out and ground in nature. Prior to the COVID-19 pandemic, humanity's overall interest in going outside and occupying the great outdoors had been declining since the 1990s. The rise of technology and social media platforms, as well as prioritizing a focus on infrastructure and architecture over the preservation of nature, contributed to this dynamic. However, when we were collectively forced to take a sacred pause, many of us discovered the healing power of nature, and it dramatically shifted our perspective on what was important to us.

So, before we go any further into this book, I want to take a moment to honor that pause with a reflection on nature and our connection to the land on which we live, work, play, and dream. This is a small yet significant way to interrupt grind culture, by making space to consider the power of nature and the legacy of the land you are on.

Assessing Your Relationship with Grind Culture

Many of us aren't even aware of our daily habits that perpetuate grind culture for ourselves and others. We may not have begun to unpack the deeper value systems and cultural inheritances that keep us stuck in cycles of harm and addiction to work. For everyone, the first and most important step is to build awareness. For this reason, I start all of my workshops and personal coaching intakes with the following assessment.

Checking in on your relationship with grind culture is essential for advocating for your mental, physical, and spiritual well-being within your professional and personal life. One of the easiest ways to tell if you are grinding is to take an honest look at your basic needs. Do you forget to eat, shower, take a walk, or get a good night's sleep? Neglecting basic needs is one of the first ways I can see grind culture manifesting in the lives of my clients. If you find yourself saying, "I haven't eaten all day," or "I haven't taken a break yet," or 'I've been sitting down all day," these are telltale signs that grind culture is dominating at the moment. I invite you now to take the following assessment yourself, to begin to see how grind culture manifests in your own life.

Record your responses to the following questions using one of these options: never, sometimes, often, or most of the time.

1. How often do you skip mealtime at work?

2. How often do you eat at your desk?

3. How often do you start working first thing in the morning (e.g., checking work emails on your phone)?

4. How often do you check work-related emails or read something for work right before bed?

5. How often do you check work-related emails after your workday is officially over?

6. How often do you feel guilty when you aren't working?

7. How often do you work three hours or more without taking a break?

8. How often do you work after your workday is officially over or on weekends?

9. How often do you feel like your work is in competition with your family?

10. How often do you miss out on family events or activities because of work?

11. How often do you feel guilty for requesting or taking time off for rest?

12. How often do you feel guilty for requesting or
    taking time off when you are sick?

If you answered "never" to eight or more of these questions, you may already be embodying a good deal of work-life liberation. If you answered "most of the time" to eight or more, you are fully immersed in grind culture. Many of us fall somewhere in the middle, and if you answered "sometimes" or "often" to the majority of these questions, you are someone who takes work seriously but has probably built in some boundaries and safeguards to protect your health and well-being. Wherever you are in this journey is okay. Remember, your value is not related to your ability to grind, and it's not related to your answers to these questions. You are whole and worthy just as you are. Changing old habits and building healing practices as you detox will not make you better or more worthy. But it can rejuvenate your life, calm your anxiety and perfectionism, and help you reclaim your wellness.

Now Breathe

After the assessment, take a moment to breathe and understand that this first step of awareness can be painful and surprising, but also know that you are stepping into a brave decision to detox from grinding. Whenever grind culture is in the driver's seat of your life, woundedness and chaos prevail. Taking the wheel back may be challenging, but joy, rest, and liberation are waiting for you on the other side.

....

Thriving Affirmation

When I move past fear to tell my story and build awareness of my present circumstances, I give others the courage to do the same.

....

Chapter 2

Grind Culture Past and Present

Not everything that is faced can be changed;
but nothing can be changed until it is faced.
—James Baldwin

Makiah Lewis is an African American mother of two girls and a Los Angeles–based accountant and tax advisor. She notes, "As soon as you get pregnant, you're Hester Prynne, from *The Scarlet Letter*. You have that Black X on your back. People are looking at you like you're disrupting the flow of the well-oiled machine of work." During her first pregnancy, Makiah worked as a bookkeeper for a manufacturing company. She was the only woman and the only Black person at the company.

"There's this unspoken perception that if you're pregnant you can't work, so you feel this pressure to always show up even when you're not feeling well," Makiah told me. "I remember working until I was thirty-nine weeks, and when it was time for me to go back to work after eight weeks, my manager said that I wasn't needed."

During her third pregnancy, Makiah was working as an account manager at an accounting firm. She recounts: "I was a person that needed a lot of help and accommodations, because I quickly found out that this was a high-risk pregnancy. I had to go to the doctor every week, and I was very tired. I had really bad blood sugar dysregulation. I was going to the bathroom frequently. At one point, I got written up because I was taking too many breaks."

Makiah kept working throughout her pregnancy despite the increasingly hostile work environment, but twenty-three days into her newborn's life, he died in her arms while Makiah was breastfeeding. Her maternity leave rapidly turned into bereavement leave. Her employer, already reluctant to provide her with maternity leave, did not grant her extended time for bereavement. Makiah chose to leave the job and took six months off work to grieve. I share this as an example of how grind culture ideals place productivity over the well-being of even the most sacred relationship—that of mother and child. I can't help but wonder, would things have been different if Makiah hadn't felt the additional stress of grind culture during her pregnancies?

Makiah's heartbreaking story is far too common among mothers in all industries and from all walks of life. But it's particularly common among African American women, and this is no accident given the long history of racial inequity in the United States rooted in slavery. As we will cover in this chapter, the dehumanization, brutality, trauma, and racism that came from slavery carries over into grind culture to this day.

Capitalism, Manifest Destiny, and Chattel Slavery

It's impossible to fully understand the enormous power and influence that grind culture has over us without examining its history and origins. In the United States, capitalism fueled the rapid growth and expansion of industry at a pace never before seen on this planet by exploiting stolen labor and stolen land.

The first slave ships landed on Turtle Island, aka "The New World" in the eyes of colonizers set on claiming it from its inhabitants, in 1619. Enslaved Africans were denied their humanity and seen as property and capital. American chattel slavery, as it has since become known, is unlike any other type of human enslavement in history. While all forms of slavery are abhorrent and inhumane, the system of slavery that grew up in the United States was even more diabolical than what the world had experienced previously in a few telling ways: First, enslaved Africans were denied their fundamental humanity and were considered property, with no legal protections of any kind regarding their treatment. Second, slavery in this case was multigenerational, meaning that all children of enslaved humans also were automatically enslaved in perpetuity. Third, and most notably, American chattel slavery was based on race. These combined factors are why psychologist and historian Dr. Joy DeGruy describes American chattel slavery as "a case of human trauma not comparable in scope, duration, and consequence with any other incidence of human enslavement."

Furthermore, these enslaved humans were all put to work on stolen land, which would later be celebrated in grind culture society under the term Manifest Destiny, a concept created by those in power in an attempt to turn thievery into chivalry. While we will never know the exact numbers, it's clear that many thousands of native peoples were either killed or forced from their homeland in the white man's quest for money and power.

With the enslavement of African people and the murder and forced relocation of Indigenous people, capitalism in the United States was able to create the fastest production schedule at the lowest possible cost. Consider for example how, shortly before the Civil War, the number one cash crop in the world was cotton, picked by enslaved humans in the American South, on land that had been previously inhabited by the Cherokee Nation and other native tribes. Tending to cotton crops was incredibly labor-intensive, but the invention of the cotton gin changed the game by creating quicker ways to process the picked cotton. Faster processing meant lower prices, which drove a need to grow and harvest at much higher rates in order to acquire wealth and power. This led to higher rates of enslavement. As labor sped up, landowners and lawmakers needed to acquire more land to keep up with demand, which in turn led to the massive land theft from Indigenous populations by the US government through military force, murder, war, and family separation. The foundation of American capitalism was built on a viciously high-stakes environment of productivity or death.

We have never had the time and space to fully process the harm done to our collective consciousness by the traumatic legacies of chattel slavery and Manifest Destiny. Yes, we need to mourn those many individual lives and legacies lost, but we also need to hold space for the psychological and emotional harm that these practices had on the American psyche. Among these harms lie many of our received attitudes around labor and productivity.

The *New York Times* 1619 Project outlines how American chattel slavery created a system of management that can still be found in multinational corporations today. Specifically, it explains that for the system of slavery to grow at such a rapid rate, it required intricate systems of control, including hierarchical structures of multilevel management and clear lines of supervision. Enslaved Africans and slave masters had quotas to meet in order to feed this vicious system of capitalism. For enslaved Africans, not meeting your quota meant facing systems of torture including whippings, starvation, and isolation. For enslaved Africans, productivity was a matter of life or death, and systems of torture increased as the prices of crops grew.

The techniques of supervision created to support American chattel slavery were developed by people who wanted to squeeze as much productivity out of their enslaved workforce in as short a time as possible. Their decisions were driven by market forces and justified by a calibrated set of values and morals that dehumanized many so that a few could profit. This is the pyramid scheme of extractive capitalism, and it persists today.

Consider sales, manufacturing, and shipping quotas; limited breaks; starvation wages; unused vacation days; and unavailable and/or unpaid family leave. In the United States, so many aspects of what we've come to normalize as commonsense, fact-of-life corporate culture is rooted in those same values. Chattel slavery is over, and yet its spirit haunts and permeates our society in multiple ways, from education to housing to finance to the prison industrial complex to voting rights. Our attitudes around work and productivity are no exception.

In many ways, grind culture is the internalized, unrealistic expectation of maximum productivity. It leads us to produce even at the expense of our overall health and well-being. It convinces us to fear the myth of scarcity above all and to view our work as our most significant accomplishment. The more productive we are, the more worthy we can hope to be in society. The ghosts of chattel slavery and Manifest Destiny haunt our spiritual and emotional lives from the inside. Breaking free of this specter requires both deep personal work and collective striving for a different kind of future.

Trauma Passed Down Through Generations

Often when we talk about the injustices of the past, some people say things like, "That's all ancient history; since *you* didn't experience slavery personally yourself, it doesn't affect you or your life directly so you should get over it." This kind of argument is problematic for several reasons. Leaving aside for the moment the fact that there is nothing "ancient" about American chattel slavery—it's something that happened in our recent past, historically speaking—there remains the fact that the repercussions of this recent history are absolutely alive and well today and continue to directly affect individuals and communities on many different levels beyond the grind culture it created—psychological, sociological, economic, etc.

In addition, scientists are now discovering that dismissing the legacy of racism and slavery as something that no longer affects those alive right now is inaccurate on a genetic level as well. Just in the last decade there have been studies in the field of epigenetics pointing to evidence that trauma can be transferred over several generations through our DNA.

We already understand how trauma can go on to affect an individual for years, as we commonly refer to things like post-traumatic stress disorder when we discuss the experiences of war veterans, refugees, or abuse survivors, among others. But the field of epigenetics is beginning to reveal that trauma moves out much further than this and can in fact affect the descendants of trauma survivors.

For example, in reviewing the health records of children whose fathers had been prisoners of war during the Civil War, researchers at the University of California in Los Angeles discovered that the sons of Civil War POWs had an 11 percent higher mortality rate than the sons of non-POW Civil War veterans—a rate that could not be explained purely through factors such as socioeconomic status. It is also significant that when the researchers compared the mortality rates and health of children born to the same men before they experienced the trauma of being prisoners of war to those born after, the sons of the same men born before the trauma of war didn't have the same mortality rates. Another study tracked the descendants of Holocaust victims and showed elevated levels of cortisol, the stress hormone, in those whose parents had suffered at the hands of the Nazi regime.

What these studies are showing us is that trauma can be passed down on a cellular level and can result in intergenerational health and mortality differences and that threats experienced by elder generations can lead to greater sensitivity to those threats in their offspring. This has enormous and obvious implications for our response to historical injustice. The emotional and physical traumas of chattel slavery and Manifest Destiny reverberate through generations, affecting individuals and communities in deep and profound ways. We have yet to discover what impact these injustices have had on our DNA.

Systemic Racism Feeds Grind Culture

Of course, the legal end of chattel slavery did not halt the racist practices and systems that made it possible. The history of Reconstruction, of voting rights in this country, of redlining, the school to prison pipeline, educational funding, lack of reparations, etc.—the effects of chattel slavery—transmuted into widespread legal, cultural, educational, and work-related racist practices that have continued to this day.

We all know that long after chattel slavery was officially ended, the United States continued to impose laws governing the bodies of Black Americans during the Jim Crow era from 1877 through the mid-1960s. Pauli Murray's book *States' Laws on Race and Color* requires 700 pages just to list all the laws related to race and skin color that were on the books until they were outlawed a half-century ago. Laws were created to lock Black people out of opportunity and keep them in a state of servitude.

In one particularly poignant example that illustrates the intersection of racism and grind culture, a 1918 city ordinance was passed in Greenville, South Carolina, requiring "free Black women" to be gainfully employed outside of their households, even if their partners were financially able to support their families. At the time, this would've applied mainly to the wives of Black men serving in World War I who were sending money home to support their families. This law mandated Black women to leave their own children and households to serve as nannies, cooks, maids, seamstresses, waitresses, etc., to support white households

and businesses. This law literally made it illegal for Black women to be stay-at-home moms.

Learning about this law, which directly attacked the rights of mothers to be with their children, shook me to my core. For women like me, Makiah Lewis, and many others, motherhood can expose us to the realities of grind culture like nothing else can.

Mothers are presented with a painful dichotomy. On one hand, we're expected to nurture our newborn from an endless well of attention, care, and presence, and on the other, grind culture wants us to prove that our caretaking won't be a liability.

When I gave birth to my son Cole, I literally felt like I was being pulled between two worlds. The simultaneous joy and helplessness that I felt during this process overwhelmed me. How was I going to be a good mother and keep grinding too?

The United States is the only country in the Americas without a national paid parental leave benefit. In Europe, the average is over twenty weeks of paid leave. Everywhere else, the average is over twelve weeks. My pregnancy was the first time I viewed my body as a liability in the workplace. I felt that producing and sustaining new life should have little or no effect on my productivity at work. Yet how could it not?

I thought of my own mother and her pregnancy journey with me. I realized that my own circumstances, as inequitable as they felt, were an improvement from her experience. She became pregnant at the age of twenty-one and worked three jobs in order to bring in the money to care for me as a single parent with a high school education. She took one week off to recuperate after my birth, and then was back at work.

As I mentioned in the last section on epigenetics, whatever stress or trauma the mother experiences can be passed down to the fetus and encoded in their foundational knowledge of the world they are preparing to enter. Racial inequity, a lack of resources for expectant mothers, and a dearth of maternity leave embedded grind culture into my DNA.

Our Personal and Collective Responsibility to Heal

As an Afro-Indigenous woman who was raised in poverty in the United States, accepting responsibility for my racial healing was a difficult idea for me to grasp. I couldn't escape my rage. I spent many years processing feelings of righteous indignation toward white Americans who thought that slavery was something that Black people just needed to "get over." I fumed at the collective wealth that white Americans had amassed all over the world from centuries of theft, murder, and rape. I spent a lot of time stewing in my anger and playing the role of the angry "woke" Black woman. My unprocessed anger and rage toward white people got in the way of my healing process and integrating my shadow self. In some ways, being angry was a shield for more complex, painful feelings. My anger also kept my focus on other people and away from the difficult internal work of healing. Eventually I realized that I needed to heal myself *for me* and no one else.

If you are a person of color, your healing journey can interrupt intergenerational trauma that was caused by your ancestors' exposure to massive amounts of violence and economic oppression. As people of color, we have a responsibility to disrupt inherited patterns of trauma so that we don't perpetuate them within our own families and communities. This might take the form of ancestral healing through altar work and communicating with your ancestors to heal past wounds. This could also look like receiving guidance and wisdom from your spiritual guardians during meditation and introspection. Your healing work might also take the form of cultural reeducation and learning about the great contributions of your culture prior to colonization as well as reclaiming ancestral spiritual practices.

To people of color who are reading this and still healing from the wounds of colonization, remember that your existence is a miracle and you were put on this earth to live a joy-filled existence. You will make the pathway easier for future generations to navigate—this is why our healing is beautifully inevitable. If trauma can be passed down via our genes, I believe joy and healing can be passed down the same way. Please know you have my full support as you take this important journey to self-healing.

Likewise, if you are a white person who is learning about white privilege and receiving training in anti-racism and allyship, you are stepping into healing as well. Just as my woke anger kept me from moving into healing, if you are dissatisfied with our country's state of affairs but feel overwhelmed or avoidant, know that it is your responsibility to reeducate yourself and your offspring to make more humane and empathetic choices to disrupt systems of oppression. Heart-centered racial allyship holds so much power.

You'll see me refer to *shadow* and *shadow work* a few times in this book. Every person, family, community, nation, and cultural group has a shadow to heal. To effectively address, heal, and transmute trauma, we'll need to engage in both individual and collective shadow work. Shadow work is a process that encourages someone to practice self-compassion while embracing the most unlovable parts of themselves. Our refusal to engage in shadow work is how interpersonal conflict shows up most of the time. When we ignore our shadow, we're able to deflect blame and accountability onto other people and outside events. Taking ownership of the solution means extreme personal growth and self-reflection.

We all have a responsibility to go into the darkness of our past and present to access healing for racial injustices and bring it forward into the world. The same is true for all of us when it comes to our relationship with grind culture.

Why Acknowledging Your Ancestral and Land-Based History Matters

In the last chapter you did a self-assessment of where you are in your relationship to grind culture. This is important work. As a complement to that, I encourage you to take this personal inventory even deeper, which entails owning/acknowledging ancestral history and the history of the land you live on. Doing the work of tapping into your ancestral and land-based history is important for several reasons:

It decolonizes our thinking. Ancestral legacies and histories can be deep, complex, and fraught; they may include traumas both personal and collective, which lead to the perpetuation of colonization in the mind and soul even after physical colonization may have ended. Knowing, naming, and owning one's ancestors begin the process of bringing these histories into the light, not only acknowledging the traumas and challenges we've inherited but celebrating the strength and power we've been given as well.

Likewise, land acknowledgments are an honest way to recognize Indigenous stewardship prior to colonization. They are an entry point in recognizing the first peoples of a place, in refusing to pretend that the history of the land we occupy either never took place at all or has no relevance to us in the present. At the same time, it celebrates the universal strength and endurance of those peoples and of the land and the earth itself.

It affirms a people's history. Ancestor acknowledgments allow us to see and name clearly the individuals who came before us, the lives they lived, and the injustices they suffered—or the injustices they inflicted on others. Land acknowledgments recognize, rather than erase, the attempted genocide of Indigenous people through generations of white supremacist policies and practices.

It provides learning opportunities. Ancestor and land acknowledgments provide rich and powerful topics of discussion and residual food for thought for the folks who experience them. By learning about ancestral and Indigenous history, we become more knowledgeable about the present world around us.

It provides intersectional conversation. Ancestor and land acknowledgments are a great way to practice courageous allyship to "the Other," i.e., communities of different races, cultures, genders, sexual orientations, etc. Likewise, it allows for the honest exploration of "the Other" within; we are, after all, never only our race, our gender expression, our religion, our sexuality. We are all complex, and those complexities can create friction within ourselves as well as with others.

Land acknowledgments are also a critical part of our healing journey in that we need to acknowledge the Indigenous stewards who have developed and practiced many spirituality practices long before Western culture was created.

I offer some guidance in creating your own ancestor and land acknowledgments below. As a reminder, pay attention to your emotional wellness as you do this work; difficult histories can bring up some powerful and overwhelming emotions. Your journal will provide a place for you to work through some of this, of course, but don't hesitate to bring deep and complicated thoughts and feelings to friends and allies or to professional counselors if you need to. Take breaks, take your time, and remember that you don't have to do everything at once.

Ancestor Acknowledgment

First it's important to discuss what I mean by *ancestors*. This word can comprise a number of different groups, including genetic, cultural, spiritual, and/or artistic ancestors. For the purposes of this book, I am using the term to refer both to genetic ancestors (i.e., family members who preceded and often directly influenced our present lives:

great-grandparents, grandparents, or parents for some) as well as cultural and community ancestors, meaning the collective cultural milieu in which our genetic ancestors lived. For example, one might consider not only a great-great-grandmother an ancestor, but also say the Gullah people and cultures in the South and the Sea Islands off the coast of the southeastern United States—and back before chattel slavery to the peoples and cultures of West Africa, from whom Gullah culture is descended—are all ancestors as well.

You may already have a working knowledge of your ancestors (and naturally if your definition of the term differs from mine please continue to use your own). If you don't, however, thanks to the internet doing this kind of research has become much easier than it might have previously been, and there are any number of websites that can help you start researching the individuals and stories of those who have come before you. However, I encourage you first to talk to any living family members who might be willing to tell you the stories they know. This practice of storytelling and authentic listening has enormous potential for healing and connection; take your time over several visits, give them the gift of your undivided attention, and grieve and celebrate their stories with them. If and when the stories are emotionally difficult, try not to shut them out—while being conscious of your own limits and needs, of course—and instead mindfully sit with feelings of sadness, fear, anger, or shame. This is a sacred conversation, even when painful; deep listening of this nature is itself one antidote to the frenetic, disconnected, story-erasing forces of grind culture.

Remember that you can always add to your ancestor acknowledgment as your knowledge grows. Don't be afraid to begin with what you know right now, no matter how slight.

The acknowledgment itself is a distillation of this knowledge into a semiformal statement. The object is to name and own the past—the place and people and culture from which you came.

Writing Your Ancestor Acknowledgment

Here are some suggested phrases to get you started:

My name is _____.

I am the daughter/son/child of _____ and _____.

My grandparents' names are _____ and _____, and they came to this country from _____.

My great-grandparents' names are

_____.

I am descended from the _____ people of _____.

I am honored to possess the strength/endurance/ wisdom of _____.

I acknowledge the pain and injustice of my ancestors in _____.

And/or: I acknowledge the injustice and pain my ancestors caused to _____.

Land Acknowledgment

Stealing land and resources, as well as the taking of Indigenous lives, served the grind of earning capital and developing the Western world. The legacy of Manifest Destiny in North America today includes an overemphasis on production no matter the human and environmental cost and extraction over the preservation and cultivation of life amid nature and communities of color.

Through land acknowledgment, we own and name this history. We recognize that balance and pausing are necessary, sacred, and restorative. We also acknowledge that the histories of a land base and the history of the people who live/lived on that land base are intertwined. We are, after all, still inhabitants of one planet only, and all of human history has happened here. To name and to understand the history and ecology of the land beneath one's feet are to grasp the profound connection of all living beings, which stands fundamentally in opposition to grind culture's elevation of production over organic life.

Writing Your Land Acknowledgment
Here are some suggested phrases to get you started:

> The name of the city/county/state/country/land I live in is _____.

> It has also been called _____ by the _____ people.

> I acknowledge and recognize the _____ people, the Indigenous communities and individuals who live here now, as well as those who were forcibly removed from their homelands.

> I affirm and honor the Indigenous sovereignty, history, language, and culture of this land.

> This land is part of the _____ ecoregion(s) (e.g., prairie, wetland, savanna, forest, etc.).

> This land and the people who live on it receive their drinking and irrigation water from
> _____.

> I acknowledge and celebrate the unique plants and animals that share this land with me, including
> _____.

Chapter 3

A Framework for Healing— Beginning the Detox Process

Insanity is doing the same thing over and over again and expecting different results.
—Unknown

I was born in the 1980s at the height of the crack epidemic in South Side Chicago. Patterns of addiction run through my family and ancestral line, and through my personal life. My father was absent due to crack addiction and mental illness. Both sets of grandparents from my mother's and father's side struggled with alcohol addiction. I myself have had experiences with food addiction and disordered eating, using both the absence and presence of food to fill a perceived void. Additionally, I grew up in the era of D.A.R.E., an antidrug program funded by the federal government to teach children and youth about the dangers of drugs. I grew up therefore with a profound awareness of addiction that was both personal and academic.

So today I find it ironic that while I was warned about drug and alcohol addiction nonstop as a child, out of all of the addictions I've been personally exposed to *work* has always been my number one drug of choice. I've always gotten a rush when performing under pressure. During college, I would push through a grueling semester and knock out all of my finals, only to fall sick the first day of my semester break. This happened like clockwork during my college experience. I prided myself on my ability to grin and bear it and considered it an accomplishment to be able to subvert the needs of my body in the name of academic excellence. I felt like I needed to do more to be seen, heard, or valued.

As I grew older and advanced in my career, this feeling persisted. Time and time again I subverted my personal needs to prove my worth and value to my employers, friends, and family members. My worth seemed to always manifest around how much I was able to produce for someone else. Finally, after the birth of my son and the summer camp experience I recounted in the introduction, I decided that another way had to be possible. I began to wonder what life would look like beyond the grind.

Decolonize Your Thinking

We've taken a look at the past history and present manifestations of grind culture. This is necessary work, as we need to understand the roots and origins of this toxic way of being before we can disentangle ourselves from it. But before we dive into the detox process, let's take some time to imagine a new world—one in which we can experience work-life liberation—and at the same time engage in practices that nourish us as sacred beings. This dreaming work is also critical; it inspires hope and gives us a vision we can turn to as we simultaneously turn away from grind culture and its seemingly overwhelming influence.

Envisioning a different world beyond grind culture and the subsequent detox process needed to get us there is all ultimately the work of *decolonization*. This term refers to the ongoing process by which a colonized people or nation reclaims sovereignty. But while decolonization can refer to political independence and/or the returning of lands to native people, the term can also be applied to a much broader process. Colonialism, as has been observed by many postcolonial thinkers, possesses much deeper and more long-term cultural and psychological implications. The Indian psychologist and social critic Ashis Nandy, for example, in his book *The Intimate Enemy: Loss and Recovery of Self under Colonialism*, is referring to these deeper implications when he says that "colonialism colonizes minds in addition to bodies and it releases forces within the colonized societies to alter their cultural priorities once and for all . . . the West is now everywhere, within the West and outside; in structure and in minds." Decolonizing from this perspective therefore refers to the rooting out of dominant, oppressive, systemic thinking; of uncovering, rejecting, and healing from the assumptions perpetuated by grind culture and its corollary dysfunctional and oppressive worldviews like patriarchy and white supremacy. It is this broader definition that I'm using here in this book.

To give an example of colonization in the workplace, the very notion of "professionalism" is a colonial construct, the idea that a person's adherence to a set of standards, code of conduct, or collection of qualities should match their acceptance within the workplace. Consequently, people who are able to "code switch" and align themselves with whiteness and wealth are usually embraced as more acceptable in the workplace. I can personally attest to this. Although I identify as a Black woman who grew up in poverty, I have been able to change my voice; and my Eurocentric name on résumés is seen more favorably in professional environments. Additionally, I benefit from light-skinned privilege, which has supported me looking more "presentable" to the colonial gaze.

Decolonizing the workplace therefore involves not only how we work but how we *think* about work, and indeed, how we think about the future of work in a post–grind culture world. We should aim to create a society in which the historically disenfranchised are not constricted by racial or gender-based systems of oppression and are instead allowed to truly *be*. Decolonization is therefore not only about uprooting and eradicating old ways of thinking, but even more critically about creating just systems where unjust systems previously existed. We know that grind culture is toxic, and decolonization acknowledges that another way is possible.

Bold visioning for the future is required to access a consciousness outside of grind culture. To decolonize our workspaces, we will need to decolonize our consciousness as well. This will be a lifelong process of unlearning and relearning.

Intersectional Wellness and Collective Care

As we begin to imagine a new course and start the process of detoxification, I want to firmly assert from the outset the truth that wellness isn't a luxury; it's a human right. Wellness, and the right to rebalance and maintain it, belongs to all of us. However, we can expand on this universal idea by going deeper to embrace the concept of *intersectional wellness,* which acknowledges that while we live in a dehumanizing grind culture system that negatively impacts the spiritual, mental, and physical wellness of everyone, it does so in greater proportion to people of color, those who identify as female, disabled folks, and other minority groups.

Intersectional wellness goes even further by affirming that everyone benefits when oppressed groups have greater access to health and wellness services as well as access to activities that support a healthy lifestyle in order to heal from the trauma of systemic oppression. It reimagines justice as a pathway toward opportunities that promote healing, rest, and joy for vibrant and diverse communities. When we're well, so are our communities. When we center intersectional wellness as our ultimate goal, we bring clarity to the ways that grind culture obscures and denies that goal for ourselves and others. When we are grinding, we perpetuate the idea that our ability to produce should supersede our overall right to health and wellness. When we divest from grind culture, we implement ample opportunities for mindfulness, flexibility, and well-being within our lives and the lives of the most oppressed among us.

Out of our understanding of intersectional wellness and decolonization in the workplace, we can then further expand our thinking about self-care into a framework of collective care. As writer and organizer Leah Lakshmi Piepzna-Samarasinha puts it,

> It's not about self-care—it's about collective care. Collective care means shifting our organizations to be ones where people feel fine if they get sick, cry, have needs, start late because the bus broke down, move slower, ones where there's food at meetings, people work from home—and these aren't things we apologize for. It is the way we do the work, which centers disabled-femme-of-color ways of being in the world, where many of us have often worked from our sickbeds, our kid beds, or our too-crazy-to-go-out-today beds. Where we actually care for each other and don't leave each other behind. Which is what we started with, right?

My pregnancy and early motherhood brought into sharp focus the need for collective care. Before then, I was partly blind to this need because of my own ableism, which is a set of practices and beliefs that assign inferior value or worth to people who have developmental, emotional, physical, or psychiatric disabilities. I noticed that I only cared about increased accommodations at work and access to rest when it impacted me on a personal level. I was guilty of the same thing I accused white people of when they were unaware of their white privilege. I was completely ignorant of my ability privilege, and learning about it for the first time made me feel awkward.

My experience as a mother showed me that I had perpetuated a trauma cycle of perfectionism through grind culture for myself and my family. I recognized the symbiotic relationship between self-care and community care. I started asking questions like, *How can we create communities of collective care and support for caregivers and vulnerable populations?*

Although pregnancy is not classified as a disability, pregnant women and disabled people share the commonality of having their ability to produce impaired, which makes them vulnerable in the workplace. Many disabled folks live with lifelong conditions that impair their ability. In her book *Care Work: Dreaming Disability Justice*, Piepzna-Samarasinha calls for disability justice to not just disrupt ableism, but to promote social justice across the spectrum. She makes the case that caring for our most vulnerable populations will lead to enhanced justice and liberation for a variety of communities.

Harnessing the essence of caring communities includes:

○ Centering human needs in the policies we create

○ Creating opportunities for rest and well-being at a systemic level

○ Investing resources in systems that help our most vulnerable populations reclaim their sovereignty and their right to thrive

When we intentionally create caring, nourishing organizations, policies, and communities, we loosen the hold that grind culture has on our consciousness. When we relinquish expectations of perfectionism of ourselves and others, we begin to heal the shadow of grind culture and create a greater sense of thriving in our work and personal lives.

The Harm Reduction Model

We've already touched on the idea that detoxing from grind culture is not going to be a one and done process, and we're not aiming to be perfect here. So I want to go a bit deeper into the framework of harm reduction, which is a public health approach used to mitigate addictive behavior and its effects. It is used when abstaining from addictive behavior is not possible or feasible. This approach accepts the person wherever they are and intervenes with the least amount of harm to the person or community. Practical strategies reduce the negative health and social consequences of the addictive behavior. Harm reduction has been an effective approach used for sexual health education and STI prevention and management, as well as a response to opioid addiction. It is strengths-based and client centered.

Harm reduction invites us to start where we are and to take baby steps toward incremental transformation. Similar to some weight loss programs, harm reduction doesn't require you to commit to an ideal body weight before beginning a lifestyle change. In harm reduction, complete abstinence is a choice to be made by the patient, not a condition imposed by a specific ideology. A basic tenet of harm reduction is respect for patients and their capacity to change.

When we embrace harm reduction when detoxing from grind culture, we reject a perfectionistic paradigm which punishes us for imperfection. Harm reduction accepts us as individuals who can transform at our own pace. Harm reduction relies on compassion and acceptance as opposed to guilt and shame.

The grind culture detox operates under a harm reduction framework. If you are living in the United States, you are immersed in the system of grind culture. It's in the air we breathe as well as within the systems that we operate in on a daily basis. An abstinence-only approach to detoxing from grind culture is not feasible for the vast majority of us, but that doesn't mean that another way isn't possible; it just means that we will need to start with compassion and acceptance and chart our own individual path.

The rest of this book details practices I've learned that are helping me and clients I work with navigate the ebbs and flows of recovering from the harm of grind culture, with exercises, questions, and journal prompts that have been developed to support individual and collective journeys to unwind our entanglements with it. As I said earlier, I am not perfect at this, and I can find myself falling into the trappings of grind culture thinking if I'm not careful. The practices that we will cover also help me to return to the center of the circle whenever I lose my balance during the ebbs and flows of life.

What do I mean by the center of the circle? For me, this is a physical feeling of presence that goes beyond whether something feels "good" or "bad." That is, I am in my own body, aware and curious, listening to myself and to those with whom I'm in relationship. I am tapped into a deep well of energy, and I feel comfortable resting and asking for help when I need or want to. When I'm in the center of the circle, I am better equipped to take care of myself and my family, to work through conflict, and to draw from my creativity and dream space. Being outside of the circle can feel like dysregulation of my body and mind, distraction, defensiveness, resentment, obsessiveness, guilt, being drawn into conflict, not holding boundaries, and people-pleasing.

By returning to the practices in this book, I know that I can reclaim my right to thriving and get my life back in alignment. I understand that any real and significant change begins with me as I turn toward the liberated future I've envisioned. My work as a workplace wellness coach, activist, and writer helps me not only refine the lens through which I view the world, but also supports me with holding up a mirror to myself as I steward people down their own pathways toward healing from grind culture. I guarantee that in some way in your life, you too are a leader—whether it's by setting an example for others in your workplace, neighborhood, or faith community, for your children, or within your friend group. I find this to be an empowering reminder: when you take responsibility for change in yourself and your own life, your healing practice ripples out into the world.

A note about spirituality: You will discern in these pages that part of my own detox process involves delving into my spiritual practice. You don't have to define your healing practice as spiritual if that doesn't vibe for you, of course, but for me it connects my detox practices with a bigger context. It reminds me that something as simple as drinking water, resting, or letting out a full belly laugh can be holy.

Core Beliefs

One of the first steps that I take when working with new clients is to examine a person's core beliefs about the human experience and their relationship to it. Core beliefs are the fundamental essence of how we view ourselves, our lives, and our future. These core beliefs are what we act upon in our lives. You uncovered some of your most basic core beliefs in the grind culture assessment, and then you may have uncovered others in your work with ancestor and land acknowledgments. If we try to implement interventions and changes without starting with the core beliefs our values are rooted in, then change will happen only at the surface level. Conversely, if we are able to excavate the root causes of our beliefs, then we can evaluate which ones serve our liberation and which ones must be transformed.

Your values around work provide a road map regarding how you internalize and push back against grind culture in your daily workflow. At the end of this chapter, you will find questions that will help excavate what your values are around work and how they impact your relationship with yourself and your colleagues. Knowing these beliefs, you can build awareness about how they show up in your grind culture journey. For example, the conditioning I received in childhood told me that work addiction was "good" while laziness was "bad." This continues to show up in my sensations and thinking, as even when I have committed to a rest period of an hour, a day, or longer, I often have to work through physical sensations of anxiety—fluttering heartbeat, agitation, racing mind—to allow myself to rest without judgment. Our core beliefs are powerful, but building an awareness practice that includes ways to interrogate those beliefs can bring profound healing. Additionally, our existing beliefs can often gracefully transform into new beliefs and values that serve our higher good, and we can integrate these into our daily lives.

One way to understand our core beliefs is to consider what we learned about our world as children from parents and caregivers. To progress in your grind culture detox journey, you will want to evaluate the values around work and productivity that you adopted in childhood, releasing those that no longer serve you and reprogramming your subconscious with new values that support your life of balance and flow.

There is a part of us that remains childlike for our whole lives—vulnerable, innocent, emotional, playful, and craving love and acceptance, There is a whole healing practice centered on acknowledging and caring for the wounds of this inner child, which I encourage you to pursue if it's appealing to you. When it comes to grind culture, it's important to remember that this childlike part of us belongs at work too, even when we're showing up as decision makers and movers and shakers. We spend a lot of time wearing masks to appear socially acceptable and to "fit in," and yet we all do better work when we're in a trusted and safe environment and when our whole self feels welcome.

When you decide to detox from grind culture, you remember parts of yourself that you've been conditioned to ignore. Here are some signs that you may be in a workplace situation that denies your wholeness:

- Fear of sharing your opinions and speaking up in meetings

- Inability to say no, leading to burnout and overwhelm

- Feeling like your work is never good enough

- Excessive people-pleasing at the expense of your mental and spiritual well-being

- Working too hard for too long and creating health problems that are then ignored

- Trying to do it all yourself and not trusting others to help you

- Lack of creativity, fear of new ideas

- Ego-driven competitiveness that stifles you and others

To be clear, these are all normal responses to a toxic workplace culture, but you may benefit from doing your own personal healing so that you can take better care of yourself; build personal power; practice setting boundaries, feeling self-compassion, and liking yourself more; and renew your spirit of creativity, curiosity, and discovery.

As we come to the end of this chapter, here is an exercise to excavate your core values around work and learn more about how your whole self can thrive.

Intention-Setting

First, set aside some time to write in your journal about your personal aspirations for this experience. What would you love to start in your life? What would be a relief to stop? What would you like to focus more on?

- I would love to start . . . (a personal writing practice, paying attention more, resting more)

- It would be a relief to stop . . . (people-pleasing, being a perfectionist, being angry all the time)

- I hope to focus on . . . (healing, dreaming, finding my passion)

Now take a moment to write down a few things you'd like to address in the long term. This is an important step, because it can take away a lot of the anxiety you might feel about things that seem far away or out of your control and free you up to focus on the present moment.

Creative Visualization

Imagine your life without grind culture:

- What would it look like?

- What would it feel like?

- How would you govern yourself throughout the day?

- How would you live your life when you're not grinding?

- What steps would have to be taken to make your dream scenario into a reality?

Your Tree of Work
This next activity asks you to consider your relationship to work and productivity as a tree, with the roots being your values, the trunk being your embodied experience, and the branches being your goals and dreams.

Take some time to meditate and/or write in your journal in response to these questions:

- What values does your family have around work? (e.g., immigrant worth ethic, a sense of entitlement, a fear of poverty, selfless service, an entrepreneurial spirit)

- How are your values today in line with or pushing against grind culture?

- What was your dream career when you were a child? Are you in alignment with that career now? Why or why not?

- How did you do in school? How has your school performance influenced your views on productivity today?

- What are your personal values around productivity? Do you have attainable goals as well as big dreams?

- What is your current work environment like? How does your body feel at the end of the day? How are you hoping to shift this in the coming year?

If you feel moved to do so, you can write words related to your responses into the shape of a tree, with the values as roots, your embodied experience as the trunk, and your hopes and dreams as the branches. Or you might want to go further and create artwork around this image with crayons, markers, or even clay or papier-mâché. Engaging through play, color, and texture can add an extra healing dimension to the exercise, particularly if you already know you engage better with color or visual art versus more abstract, "wordy" material.

....

Thriving Affirmation

I honor and respect my whole self by listening to my feelings, accepting my shadows, and honoring my dreams.

I am sovereign, liberated, and free.

....

Chapter 4

Reclaiming Rest

We humans have lost the wisdom of genuinely resting and relaxing. We worry too much. We don't allow our bodies to heal, and we don't allow our minds and hearts to heal.
—Thich Nhat Hanh

In West African spiritual traditions, Nana Buluku is the mother goddess of all creation. She is the grandmother of the orishas in the Ifa tradition of West Africa and the Caribbean and a powerful symbol of the symbiotic relationship of rest and power. She gave birth to the divine twins Mawu (the moon) and Lisa (the sun), who in turn created the universe. These twins also represent the balance of the universe, the yin/dark/female/softness and yang/light/male/strength of the West African cosmology. Notably, after their birth, Nana Buluku retreated to the heavens, declining to participate in the ordering or governing of the world. Instead, she rested.

Nana Buluku's creation story portrays the essence of less is more. Her one powerful act created the universe, and that was more than enough. As such, Nana Buluku teaches us that rest is a gateway for healing and power. As we move through this chapter, consider the symbol of Nana Buluku and the mantra attached to her legacy: *She rests to create.*

Rest is critical to any healing work we do in mitigating the harmful effects of grind culture. Know of course that I am not saying that all forms of grinding are destructive. Sometimes you do need the power of initiation, quick action, followed by steadfastness to accomplish a worthy goal. Our passion projects often deserve or require a burst of energy and commitment that allows us to push through in the short term. In this way it might be helpful to think of our work cycles in terms of nature or plant cultivation. There are times for seeding, watering, and harvest, and then there are times of allowing the earth to rest. Some seasons are naturally busier than others.

The problem, therefore, isn't busyness per se, but rather the fact that because we have so much access to work all the time, and much of our work is not related to seasonal phases as it would've been in agrarian societies, it all becomes a blur of nonstop, high performance output. We are told, in hundreds of ways, in endless variation, that if we can be producing, we should be producing. We get this message from market forces, bosses, family members, and the media. Somewhere along the way, we forgot how to stop. We became afraid of rest.

Even our rest time is cluttered with information to digest, decisions to make, and a barrage of images and sound bites hitting us all day and all night. We live in a distraction economy that fights for our attention and keeps us busy. We are inundated with technological devices, advertising, and social media memes and videos on platforms that were designed to keep us addicted to being online. We've become so used to the noise that a not-so-small part of us is afraid of being alone with ourselves and our thoughts. We are fearful of being still long enough to truly sit with ourselves. If we're still long enough, then an unpleasant memory may arise or a part of our shadow self may show up and we'll need to contend with it. In this distraction-filled society, stillness can be downright scary. Sometimes it's easier to be on autopilot than to pause and rest.

This lack of authentic rest isn't only a matter of our individual wellness; our lack of sleep is a real public health issue, and grind culture deserves its share of the blame. How many of us have heard the phrase, "I'll sleep when I'm dead"? Or been encouraged to push through the need to rest in order to produce and then applauded for it when we do so?

Because of these messages, it can be hard to wrap our heads around the importance of sleep. Because we favor and prioritize our conscious minds and our waking life, most of us don't really understand how important sleep is on a physical, neurological, and spiritual level. There are so many brain tasks, for example, that can only take place in our deepest cycles of sleep, which precede the REM or dreaming cycle. These tasks include synthesizing short-term memory into long-term memory, repairing structures in the brain, growing neurons, and more. If we don't spend enough time in deep sleep states, we decrease our ability to learn, have trouble repairing our cells and muscles, and dysregulate everything from emotions to appetites.

Furthermore, lack of sleep can lead to chronic illnesses such as depression, high blood pressure, compromised immunity, and migraines, just to name a few. When we make proper time for sleep and restorative practices, it helps us to fight off diseases and restore nutrients, and it increases our spiritual and emotional health and well-being so that we're able to thrive. By design, one-third of a person's life should be spent at rest.

Because we as a society see work as the highest good, the more productive we are, the more worthy we are told we are. In this model, rest and sleep can only slow us down in our pursuit of work. Grinding has been glorified as being the way to get things done. But grind culture and toxic productivity are not only harming us individually in the short term, they are also keeping us in cycles of trauma and oppression as a society.

In order to work toward a socially just society and reclaim our individual wellness, reclaiming rest is a must. Rest is foundational to healing from grind culture. The good news is that there are many ways to integrate different types of rest into our workday and our homelife. The end of this chapter includes rituals to promote healthy sleep and intentional rest. Let's take a closer look at the science and history of sleep and its connection to productivity.

The Sleep Gap

Grind culture has convinced us that resting slows productivity, and therefore that we are right to disregard our own humanity and our bodies' basic needs in order to excel, or even just keep up. As a result, our collective sleep patterns have become gravely interrupted. According to the Sleep Foundation, the average adult needs seven to nine hours of sleep each night in order for our bodies to function at optimum health.

The data show that issues such as race and income can impact your overall quality of sleep in the United States. Insufficient sleep is considered to be a public health threat, and the CDC reported that in 2016 more than one-third of Americans were not getting enough sleep. Additionally, the CDC reported that sleep outcomes were severely impacted by race, with only 54 percent of African Americans and 60 percent of Native Americans getting a healthy allotment of sleep. People who were unable to work or were otherwise unemployed also received less sleep, with 51 percent of this population obtaining healthy sleep outcomes. Additionally, Tuck.com wrote an article tracking job roles and sleep quality among 35,000 business leaders and found a correlation between sleep quality and job type. "The more senior their role, the more that person sleeps, with senior executives getting the most sleep of all. Considering that senior executives also tend to have extremely high household incomes, these results support the broader trend that financial security goes hand in hand with better sleep."

With grind culture holding the steering wheel of our economy and business structures, it makes sense why people with less access to wealth would have a difficult time sleeping. With the increase of gentrification and the rising cost of living in American cities, 15 percent of the American workforce works multiple jobs. These folks are 61 percent more likely to sleep less than six hours on a weeknight, since increased time is spent working and commuting to multiple jobs. When working multiple jobs, people are more likely to have irregular work hours, begin work earlier, and end it later, preventing them from following a regular sleep schedule.

Additionally, people of color are more likely to experience political phenomena such as redlining, a discriminatory practice that puts services (financial and otherwise) out of reach for residents of certain areas based on race or ethnicity. The process of redlining can prevent Black people and other folks of color from living in higher-resourced areas, which are typically predominately white due to the racial caste system in America. Research shows that living in poorer areas can lead to less sleep as well. They're typically crowded, which means more light pollution and a noisier living space.

Tricia Hersey has created a body of work around deprogramming grind culture. Hersey founded the Nap Ministry as a movement created to disrupt grind culture, white supremacy, and capitalism in the United States. Drawing on her background as a performance artist, theater maker, activist, theologian, and community healer, she promotes the Nap Ministry message through rest demonstrations and social media education.

When I first heard about the Nap Ministry, I chuckled and thought it sounded funny and witty, and yet her words spoke to me at a spiritual level. The Nap Ministry makes the connection between the roots of slavery in the United States and how it has impacted the American psyche when it comes to work and productivity. Grind culture impacts anyone and everyone, regardless of gender, race, or social class. However, as we have explored, it can impact you on a deeper level if you are a person of color.

Hersey reminds us by way of her research, teachings, quotes, and public performances that we are not machines and we were not meant to grind. For her, rest is a form of reparations. We must reclaim our rest.

The Legacy of Dream Temples

Ancient African civilizations held a great deal of wisdom about the science of sleep and its positive impact on our spiritual, mental, and emotional well-being. In ancient Egyptian times, dreams were used to cure disease. When the ancient Egyptians had a physical or emotional ailment, they went to what were called sleep temples (also known as dream temples), which were not places of worship and prayer, but particularly for healing. In ancient Egypt, sleep was linked to death and the afterlife because in both instances, the person was being transported into another realm. Sleep temples existed in North Africa, the Middle East, and ancient Greece. They were known to be places for regeneration, solace, and restoration. These temples were one of the earliest documented cultural practices of using hypnotic states for healing. Hypnosis is a trance-like state that resembles sleep and can be self-initiated or induced by a therapist or healing practitioner. Today, there is a growing body of scientific research that details the benefits of hypnosis in treating a wide variety of ailments. In ancient Egypt, priests were viewed as physicians and sleep temples as clinics.

The temple of Imhotep and the Step Pyramid at Saqqara were important healing centers in the late third century BCE and utilized the element of sleep to cure problems and ailments. Imhotep, whose name means "he who comes in peace," was the first physician recorded in history and the architect of the first pyramid. He was known as a polymath, a person of wide-ranging knowledge and learning, similar to Benjamin Franklin or Leonardo da Vinci.

Imhotep's legacy lives on today. He was so influential that Sir William Osler, one of the founders of Johns Hopkins Hospital, referred to Imhotep as "the first figure of a physician to stand out from the midst of antiquity." Imhotep is also considered to be the great-grandfather of hypnotherapy; he performed his medical treatments in sleep temples and induced trancelike states in his patients to promote healing.

Years after his death, ancient Egyptians worshipped him and frequented sleep temples in his honor. The sleep temple experience would consist of patients being put into a trance through ingesting herbs, reciting incantations, meditating, and repeating mantras for a period of several hours. Next, the patient would be led to a sleep chamber to receive a healing message from the dream world. The process of healing through dreams was called dream incubation and involved sleeping in a temple for the purpose of receiving a dream to promote healing. Dream incubation was one of the most popular healing modalities in Ancient Egypt. ancient Egyptians viewed resting as serious business.

Decolonizing Rest

Although the practice of sleep temples continued on for some time in the Middle East and Greece, the practice gradually died out with the spread of Christianity, which disseminated colonial beliefs that viewed such ritualistic practices as unholy and sacrilegious. Unfortunately, colonization has led to many African-centered healing traditions being lost due to fear, mistrust, and prejudice. The loss of sleep temples is a product of this colonization, and we can decolonize sleep and bring dream-based healing practices back into our lives. Whenever possible, we can reclaim Indigenous- and African-centered ways of knowing and integrate them into our wellness practices. The new age spirituality market owes many of its tools and much of its knowledge to African, Eastern, and Indigenous traditions.

Sankofa is a West African phrase that means, "It is not taboo to fetch what is at risk of being left behind." Much of the work that we are doing as we detox from grind culture is reclaiming ancestral wisdom in order to propel us into a brave future of increased thriving and well-being. Now's the time to reclaim all of what has been lost. In this reclamation, we will also find our power.

Education researcher Eve Tuck discusses how "whitestream voices are constructed as rigorous, logical, reasoned, and valid while voices outside of the whitestream are considered experiential and emotional, representing devalued ways of knowing." The adoption of Western constructs such as capitalism, colonization, and grind culture has led us to the inhumane speed that we are currently racing in. The dominant culture sees these constructs as commonsense, normal, or logical without interrogating them. Is it really "normal" to sacrifice our bodies to profit someone else? Is it logical to deny our biological needs? Clearly not. Now is the time to pause, and then go back and fetch ancient wisdom that was lost, but not quite forgotten. It's time to reclaim our understanding of the value of a well-rested society.

The Seven Types of Rest

Healthy sleep patterns provide a gateway to thriving. Contrary to popular belief, sleep is an active time during which we process information, restore our energy levels, and repair our tissues and biological systems. Sleep is one important aspect of rest, but there are more ways to access this essential nourishment. Dr. Saundra Dalton-Smith opens up the more poetic aspects of this practice when she says, "Rest speaks peace into the daily storms your mind, body, and spirit encounter. Rest is what makes sleep sweet."

Dalton-Smith is an Alabama-based board-certified internal medicine physician and an award-winning author and speaker on topics related to mental health and work-life integration. She situates sleep in a larger context of rest and focuses on integrating a holistic perspective for individuals to get proper rest for enhanced well-being. In her book *Sacred Rest: Recover Your Life, Renew Your Energy, Restore Your Sanity*, she calls for a "rest revolution," and highlights the seven types of rest we need in order to thrive:

○ Physical rest

○ Mental rest

- Emotional rest

- Spiritual rest

- Social rest

- Sensory rest

- Creative rest

Many of these are self-explanatory—we intuitively know how to get physical, mental, and emotional rest. Spiritual rest refers to practices that enhance your connection to your spiritual or religious beliefs and values. Social rest means taking time to recover from the stimulation of social interactions. Sensory rest involves quieting the stimulus overload on your five senses. Creative rest refers to ways that you can daydream, doodle, dance, or play without a specific mandate to produce or achieve anything. Often, one type of activity can provide a respite for another rest category. For example, going on a long hike may not be physically restful, but it can give your overthinking mind a mental break and renew your emotional state. Connecting with loved ones may provide spiritual rest, even though you're being socially active.

Dalton-Smith says, "Most people, when they think about rest, they have a very one-sided approach—they lounge around, don't do anything, and think that's what rest is. . . . We try it, and then when we're still rest-deprived, we think [resting] doesn't work." According to Dalton-Smith's research, once you understand your rest deficit, along with the types of rest you need, you're able to create a plan that supports sleep and overall wellness. Just as you wouldn't change your diet and exercise plan without assessing your current reality, it's important to know where you stand in terms of rest.

I took Dr. Dalton-Smith's rest quiz when I was trying to reclaim rest in my personal life during the first year of the COVID-19 pandemic. With heavier time on screens, balancing my home and work life with a toddler, and coparenting with my husband, who often works the night shift as an emergency responder, my sleep was disrupted and I was looking for tools to reclaim healthy rest cycles. After taking the quiz, I learned that I needed to modify my rest patterns to get more physical and sensory rest. This included stepping up my leisure walks, integrating more stretching throughout the day, drinking more water first thing in the morning, and sleeping between six and eight hours per day.

Sensory Rest in a Digital Age

As for sensory rest, this aspect of my life has been more difficult to tackle because of the amount of time I was spending on screens during my work and personal life. My visual and audio perception were on all the time, while my senses of touch, smell, and taste fell into the background, underused and out of balance. Some of the ways Dr. Dalton-Smith recommended getting sensory rest included spending dedi-cated time each day off technology, spending more time in silence, eating fruits and vegetables in their raw state, sleeping in a cool, dark room, and adjusting the brightness settings on my devices.

Another way I began to promote sensory rest within my workday was to take more phone appointments as opposed to being on Zoom for every meeting. When so much of the working population was forced to go remote during the pandemic, many workplaces went into a trauma response of overscheduling video meetings to make up for the loss of in-person connection. But we didn't account for the stress of being on screens all day, which can include poor sleep quality. Staring at screens can even lead to screen apnea, a term coined by technologist and consultant Linda Stone, during which a person holds their breath while scrolling, watching, or otherwise looking at screens. The brain processes looking at ourselves differently than look-ing at others in a conversation. Looking at ourselves while we are talking, as we do on many video conferences, is extra taxing for the brain and adds yet another cognitive task to our remote workdays. One way to mitigate this is to turn off "self-view" so that the visual experience more closely mirrors an in-person conversation.

In our highly digitized world, there's this pressure to be "on" all of the time. Grind culture no doubt benefits from our phones and computers being quite literally attached to our bodies or within reach constantly. We are almost always accessible to bosses, clients, and employees. There is no excuse for not working nonstop, and if we do make time to power down and rest, we might be seen as difficult or unreliable. Being offline has become a luxury only a few can afford.

This dynamic is supported by the design of the technology that we use on a daily basis. According to Charles Czeisler of Harvard Medical School, "Artificial light exposure between dusk and the time we go to bed at night suppresses release of the sleep-promoting hormone melatonin, enhances alertness, and shifts circadian rhythms to a later hour—making it more difficult to fall asleep." As an executive leader of a nonprofit organization in a time of deep crisis and pain, I struggled to reclaim my sensory rest. The pressure to be on made it difficult to put my phone down.

I'm not alone in that feeling. Nomophobia, or NO MObile PHone PhoBIA, is a term used to describe a psychological condition when people have a fear of being away from cell phone connectivity. Have you ever left your phone at home accidentally and felt a physical sensation, a kind of anxious inner tug? According to Trend Hunter, 66 percent of the world's population suffers from phone addiction—and the numbers are rising each year. Digital devices aren't going anywhere, but as I hope you can see, they are also dangerously harmful to our health if overused.

On the flip side, as harmful as these devices have been to our health, having access to them has also created pathways to greater knowledge and information than we've ever thought possible. By no means am I suggesting to completely get rid of cell phones; however, we can employ a harm reduction process to circumvent the damage that's being caused by these devices to our bodies, minds, and spirits.

I decided to focus on finding ways to promote sensory rest through more time intentionally off devices. I've installed social media blocking apps to ensure that I stay off social media platforms for set periods of time, such as over the weekend. I noticed that when I forced myself off social media, I was able to engage in other activities that fed my spirit, whether that was yoga, taking a hike, reading, or writing. Giving my eyes analog breaks has been helpful on my journey to reclaiming sensory rest and circumventing the impact of screen apnea. It has also awakened my other senses and rebalanced my overall sensory experience.

Using the information gathered from Dr. Saundra Dalton-Smith's rest quiz, I was able to cultivate additional practices to counteract the increased screen time inherent in working remotely. I added these to my personal thriving tool kit, refined them with my staff at the time, and shared them with my clients when I opened my coaching practice. Here they are, in case they are helpful to your own thriving tool kit.

Thriving tips for working remotely:

Incorporate a morning and/or nightly ritual. This is your time to reconnect with your personal values, vision, and purpose, and it will ground you in your why and help you to show up as the best version of yourself for your day ahead.

Make room for sacred time. A simple neck roll, mindful breathing exercise, or check-in with your body can go a long way. Aim for three ten-minute sessions per workday.

If possible, limit the number and duration of video meetings. If you must meet on video frequently or for long periods of time several days a week, consider going off screen or taking an audio call rather than a full video meeting.

If you can, schedule a break between meetings. This gives you time to restore yourself and take care of your body's needs.

Creative Rest

Another kind of rest that deserves to be engaged with in depth is creative rest. Creativity is a fundamental human impulse and a human need. While many people may insist that they "are not creative," the truth is that human beings are by nature creative. Creativity, like wellness, is our birthright. Whenever we are engaged in creative activities that are free from the pressure of competition and productivity, we are engaging in creative rest.

When we are at rest creatively, we naturally enter a state of flow, which psychologist Mihaly Csikszentmihalyi defined as "optimal experience" in his best-selling book *Flow: The Psychology of Optimal Experience*. This is a state in which all parts of our being—body, mind, and soul—feel as though they are working together in tandem, without any sense of stress or pressure. This state can be a key to cultivating greater overall happiness and a sense of purpose and inner peace.

While most people automatically think of the arts as synonymous with creativity, the fact is that creativity covers a much broader range of human experience. Even if you don't consider yourself to be creative, you most likely are—just in a field you may not think of as creative right away. Building, cooking and baking, decorating, community organizing, web design, arranging seasonal altars, food preservation, and hair and makeup design are just a few creative endeavors, as are writing, dancing, acting, singing, painting, drawing, and sculpture.

Creative rest specifically happens when exploration is divorced from the pressure to produce, or from the pressure to create something "valuable" or "good." These are arbitrary measures anyway, but we can go even further to consider what it means to engage our creativity entirely outside of these terms. When we do, we find that we might be drawn toward activities that we have shunned all our lives out of an insistence that we are "not good at it." What would it mean for you, for example, if you painted something without worrying about whether it was "any good" or not? Perhaps you've always wanted to write poetry but have been "sure" it would be terrible. But when viewed solely as a *practice*, as something to engage in for pure enjoyment over the final product, without need for scrutiny, assessment, or judgment, artistic endeavors become instead a source of play, joy, and . . . rest!

If you already have a creative practice, consider this a friendly reminder to make some time for it on a regular basis. For those who don't yet have a chosen creative medium, there is a world of possibility out there for you! Even ten to twenty minutes of creative rest can be rejuvenating. Activities like sketching, doodling, writing poetry, or painting small abstracts in acrylic or watercolor take very little time and few materials to get started. And don't be afraid to play—some of your favorite activities from childhood, like using Play-Doh, crayons, or magnetic sand, may be fantastic outlets for some creative rest. And these of course are just within the category of arts and crafts. Remember that spending time in the kitchen trying out a new complicated recipe, arranging/refreshing a seasonal altar, or rearranging a living space can be just as relaxing if that's your creative practice of choice.

The Resource of Time

When I first present these thriving tips to my clients, anxiety comes up around the feasibility of executing such a plan. The truth is, we can all invite more opportunities for rest into the workday if we reimagine our relationship with time. Traditionally in Western society, time is seen as a scarce resource, and yet it's a construct in which we all participate. That doesn't mean time is not real—it is—but we have more ability to flip the narrative than we might think. When I map out my calendar, I choose to see my time as abundant. I intentionally overestimate the amount of time it will take me to complete certain tasks in order to provide more spaciousness and flow within my workday. This is a thriving practice, a process-based approach. When we are operating from the system of grind culture, we are working against the clock to get everything done. Even this wording leads to the imagery of struggling and fighting with time to accomplish a fixed goal. The truth is that no matter how hard we work, there's always more work to be done. Time management is about priorities and choosing where we focus our energy. Once we reframe our relationship with time and see time as abundant and expansive, we can let go of the struggle and create more opportunities for rest in our lives.

An Emergent Strategy Approach to Time and Work

In November 2019, I attended the Emergent Strategy Ideation Institute (ESII), hosted by adrienne maree brown, author of the book *Emergent Strategy*. Emergent strategy is a pattern of action that develops over time in an organization in the absence of a specific mission and goals. Seeking alternative leadership approaches after my time at the nonprofit summer camp I ran, I found the workshop's relationship to time and productivity to be a huge and inspiring paradigm shift.

At the ESII workshop there was no agenda, and it was up to the participants in the training (as well as a tarot deck) to guide ourselves on our learning journey. We didn't learn skills and terms, but rather dove directly into creating the conditions for transformative learning, growth, and development to emerge in an organic and life-affirming way. Everything was cocreated on the spot within our training space, with brown's "Less Prep, More Presence" mantra echoing in our heads. ESII taught me how to appreciate and seek to understand nonlinear organizational approaches— a revolutionary shift from product-based work to process-based work.

The participants split into smaller groups based on our common interests, and we were each tasked with creating and facilitating an experience for the larger group. I joined a group focused on healing. We had very little time to prepare, less than I would ever give my perfectionist self to create something new, and yet we came together, learning how to work with each other in a very quick way with only the tarot card we pulled as our guide. We cocreated a collective rest ceremony. The time and space we needed seemed to open up for us as we focused on the process, and not on creating a perfect, final, or definitive product.

The speed, vitality, and success of this rest ceremony were gratifying. Although I had been toying with the idea of cofacilitating rest sessions for the greater public, I struggled to see myself as a "real" healer and was sure I was lacking in the skills. After all, wasn't it only a few months ago that I had been running myself ragged and engaging in modes of sleep deprivation in the name of social justice healing?

During the collective rest portion of our training, I read the following quote by the Nap Ministry: "I ain't hustlin' for nothing. I am enough now AND my ancestors already laid the path for my liberation and progress. I am resting."

It was a definitive, full circle moment. Resting felt like defiance after spending so many years of my adult life sacrificing the needs of my body, mind, and spirit in order to produce. This is the importance of rest. It disrupts grind culture's spinning wheels. There is power in the slowdown. When you slow down, you rest; when you rest, you self-reflect; when you self-reflect, you begin to question, which in turn disrupts the culture of grinding.

Time and work changed for me during this workshop. I believe you too can access creativity and collaboration much more quickly than you might imagine if you release the burden of perfectionism. I also believe that you deserve to carve out space to rest as an act of rebellion.

Black Healing and Rest

I was hungry to create more of these experiences where I felt like I could become a glitch in the system of grind culture, and cofounded Black Healers Connect, a digital and in-person hub for Black healers to reclaim ancestral wisdom for personal and community thriving.

We hosted an event on February 22, 2020, called Rest as Ritual, opening up a portal for ease and rest with yoga nidra, sound healing, a tea ceremony, collective rest, and a healing circle. It was the first event of its kind: an all-Black sound healing in West Oakland at a Black-owned yoga studio called Yoga Love in a country where Black people have some of the poorest quality of rest in the nation. We were quiet, but our resistance was no less powerful.

In his book *The Sovereignty of Quiet*, Kevin Quashie describes the power of quiet within Black social justice movements:

> Resistance may be deeply resonant with black culture and history. But it is not sufficient for describing the totality of black humanity. The idea of quiet is compelling because the term is not fancy. It is an everyday word, but it is also conceptual. Quiet is often used interchangeably with silence or stillness . . . Quiet instead is a metaphor for the full range of one's inner life, wants, desires, ambitions, hungers, vulnerabilities, fears, the inner

life is not apolitical or without social value. But neither is it determined entirely by publicness. In fact, the interior dynamic and ravishing is a strike against the dominance of the social world. It has its own sovereignty, it is hard to see, even harder to describe, but no less potent and it's inevitable.

The quiet and intuitive moments that rest can bring threaten grind culture's desire to produce at all costs. When we honor rest, we honor our bodies and our processes over the product. In the eyes of grind culture, a well-rested society is considered dangerous. Recall the ordinance that forced Black mothers to work outside the home. In a society that profits from us being sleep-deprived, it is our responsibility to become vigilant about reclaiming our rest.

Restoring your connection to rest practices is a powerful individual practice that can yield collective results. Like emergent strategy, the success of your rest practice will be nonlinear, iterative, and created moment by moment. Trust the process. Here are some strategies you can incorporate to reclaim your rest and promote thriving in your work and personal life.

Tools for Reclaiming a Restful Night's Sleep

- Sleep with an eye mask, blackout curtains, and white noise.

- Sleep next to a diffuser and use lavender or other essential oils that promote rest.

- Purchase detox foot pads infused with bamboo vinegar and essential oils.

- Place a small water fountain near your bedside.

- Sleep with your phone in the other room. (If your nomophobia is really bad, then play some white noise or binaural beats through your phone and put on an eye mask to give your eyes a break.)

- Take an Epsom salts bath with lavender a couple hours before bedtime.

- If you live in a place where it is legal to do so, you can try products with CBD to support relaxation and anxiety relief.

- Take melatonin, a hormone created by the pineal gland that lets your body know when it's time to sleep.

- Invest in good bedding and soothing, calm colors in your room. Your sleeping area should embody the rest that you seek as much as possible.

Promote Rest in Your Workday with Bees' Breath

This humming sound and breath exercise will renew your connection to your breath, and it is especially helpful if you're prone to holding your breath or screen apnea.

Start by taking a few natural breaths, and close your eyes—as long as closing them doesn't produce more anxiety. Plug your ears and cover your eyes with your remaining fingers on each side. Then, keeping the lips lightly sealed, inhale through the nostrils. Exhaling, make the sound of the letter M or a humming sound. Breath in for four breaths, hold for two, and exhale for six breaths. Do this for a total of seven repetitions at a time.

Self-Care Assignment: Take a Nap

Experiment with taking a twenty- or thirty-minute nap between the hours of one and six p.m. This will help provide you with a jolt of energy. Naps or periods of intentional rest such as yoga nidra or meditation can enliven and deepen your daily routine and rebalance some of the various rest deficits you are probably experiencing within grind culture.

Thirty- to ninety-minute naps can improve memory and brain cognition. But note that sleeping more than ninety minutes during a nap can have the opposite effect, as rousing from the deeper sleep cycles can leave you groggy and uncoordinated.

You might need to be creative about where you take your nap. It might need to be in your car or at your desk. If you can manage it, try to lean into a nap during your lunch break.

Just as you consider adding breaks between meetings in your day, consider putting a nap on your calendar. It might feel silly at first, but rest is an act of resistance and healing.

....

Thriving Affirmation

Rest is necessary for my well-being.

....

Chapter 5

Self-Care Through Somatics and Sound

The earth cannot move without music. The earth moves in a
certain rhythm, a certain sound, a certain note. When the music
stops the earth will stop and everything upon it will die.
—Sun Ra, *Space Is the Place*

While essential, rest alone won't allow us to fully detox from grind culture in the way that we so desperately need. In this chapter, we will look at specific healing tools you can use throughout the day to reclaim your life at work and beyond. These tools will be grounded in self-care.

As I mentioned earlier, grind culture tells us that self-care is a luxury when in fact it is a human right. That bears repeating: You don't need to earn the right to take care of yourself. You are already worthy of care and attention. This is your birthright.

When we collectively reject the narrative that self-care is a luxury, we activate liberatory rest for groups who have historically suffered from systemic oppression. When we value wellness as real work, we affirm that when we are well, we contribute to the wellness of our communities by showing up as our embodied selves while inspiring others to do the same. When our bodies and minds are well, we are able to engage in our work from a much more effective and impactful space.

One of the ways I teach others that we can engage in self-care and detox from grind culture is through somatic practices. This term will be new for some of you, so let me take a moment to define it here. Somatic practice is the art of learning how to listen to your body as it moves or to become aware of what you feel and where you feel it. Doing so can help you find places of pain, discomfort, or dis-ease that are often dismissed as unimportant by the thinking mind.

A trademark of colonization and grind culture is placing primary importance on logic-based thinking, as this is considered the most valuable skill in a Eurocentric worldview. Of course, it's this very logic-based thinking that created grind culture in the first place, originally by justifying the use of stolen labor and stolen land to maximize profits, and later by transferring the slave driver mentality to our current workplace culture while simultaneously creating the largest environmental disaster in history. All of this was done and justified by logic, and in the name of faster, cheaper production.

While there is certainly a place for logic-based thinking in a balanced human, grind culture's overemphasis on it has tipped the scale in the other direction and dismissed the wisdom of the body, which in many ways is an extension of our subconscious minds. For instance, as you read this, your heart is pumping life-giving oxygen via the circulatory system to all parts of your body; your digestive tract is processing the energy that Mother Earth has provided; and your cells are working to repair any areas that have been damaged. All of these things are occurring without the help of the logic-based thinking mind, but they are critical when it comes to your health and wellness.

Returning to somatics, these are practices that get us out of our heads and into our bodies to bring balance to the whole. At work, the benefits are clear. Incorporating somatic practices during your workday can help you reclaim your sovereignty. The practices that will be shared in this chapter don't take long—even five minutes can provide you with an energetic reset and build your resilience, as all of these practices assist in moving around stagnant energy.

I'm particularly passionate about people of color reclaiming these wellness practices within our personal and professional lives. As a Black woman, I've been lucky to live in the Bay Area where people of color access alternative healing modalities at higher rates and are more open to healing methods not yet supported by things like Western medicine and that exist outside of the traditional Christian narrative.

When I consider my evolution as a healer, much of my healing journey has been in unlearning the stigma and taboos that exist around African spirituality in American culture. Learning about the African origin of many of the healing modalities reignited my connection to the wisdom of my ancestors and allowed me to reclaim their medicine. Once I was able to see myself in these healing practices, to embody them, they became more real for me and felt more accessible.

It's not enough to believe that grind culture is toxic and needs to change; we will want to engage in daily actions that match our beliefs and prove that another way of approaching work is in fact possible. In order for us to reclaim our well-being as well as our right to thrive in our professional lives, we want to embody a way of life that exists outside of grinding.

Our bodies are constantly communicating to us through sensations, informing us of our physical and spiritual needs—but many of us don't know how to listen. In grind culture, we aren't given the opportunity to make space or pause long enough to listen to the sacred information that our bodies hold for us. Although our bodies are our first lived experience on this earthly plane, we're trained to honor our intellect above all else.

Somatic practices are critical in reminding us that the mind, body, and spirit share a symbiotic relationship with one another. When we begin navigating the world while listening to our bodies, our perspective shifts.

As someone who's been impacted by high-functioning anxiety for most of my life, I have historically been afraid of stillness and quiet. The idea of being alone with my thoughts was scary, and for a while, I lacked the tools to regulate my emotions and to make space for mindfulness. I was afraid to sit with myself and spent a lot of time feeling nervous about the possibility of future catastrophic events. I lacked the language as well as the tools to see that another way of existing could be possible. It wasn't until I read Bessel van der Kolk's groundbreaking book *The Body Keeps the Score: Brain, Mind, and Body in the Healing of Trauma* that I began to rethink the relationship I had with my body.

Van der Kolk makes a compelling argument about the benefit of somatics and body-based practices when healing from trauma and thriving in personal and professional settings. When you grow up in a traumatic environment, or if you are living within what is known as a persistent traumatic stress environment, or PTSE, incorporating mindfulness practices in your life becomes that much more essential. When you are healing from trauma or PTSE, learning how to make friends with your body through listening, care, and attention will ease your path.

You can make friends with your body through somatic practices, whether they're focused on mental awareness (meditation, therapy), kinesthetic experience (body scans, free movement, massage, Alexander Technique) or spiritual state (prayer, chanting, ritual). Many practices incorporate levels of somatic experiencing at the same time, like yoga, ecstatic dance, sound healing, and many more. Somatic practices are a form of self-love. They are rooted in the self, in your subjective experience of your body. When you care for your body, you assert that you matter and that you are of value. In a society that consistently ignores the sovereignty of the body through systems that perpetuate perfectionism, grind culture, and white supremacy, caring for your body is a revolutionary act. Being in tune with your body through practices like yoga and mindfulness supports your mental health and well-being as well as builds a healthy and resilient relationship with productivity.

The Healing Benefits of Yoga

Cameo Turner is an Oakland-based yoga practitioner who was diagnosed with depression at the age of sixteen. Prior to her career in yoga, she was a construction worker for fifteen years. As an African American female working in an industry dominated by white males, the stressful dynamics of her job led her to bouts of anxiety and further depression, but the final straw was when she discovered a lump on her breast.

Cameo was fearful for her well-being and the future of her kids. She knew that she needed to relax, destress, and take care of her mind and body, but she was unsure of what that path would look like for her. She had friends who encouraged her to try yoga, but she was very resistant. "Everybody kept trying to get me to do yoga, so I could let out my emotions, but I was terrified. I thought I was going to die. I have two kids and was trapped in fear-based thoughts. One day a friend of mine was like, 'Let's do yoga.' And I was like, 'Nope, that's a white people thing.' I kept resisting until one day she was like, 'You want to smoke weed and do yoga?' That sounded fun, so I said yes. She let me borrow Dee Dussault's *Ganja Yoga*. At first I brushed the book off, but by the end of my first ganja yoga session, I was hooked. Before that moment, I never saw my space in the world of wellness, but once I was able to connect yoga with weed, then my yoga journey began."

Cameo soon became the first certified Black Ganja Yoga practitioner in the Bay Area, and worked to carve out a space for herself that supported her healing and well-being. Cameo states, "When I started my yoga training, I only wanted to do it for myself. I never planned on teaching. I couldn't see myself as a yoga teacher because I saw most yoga studios as whitewashed. I felt uncomfortable. I didn't feel safe in those spaces. One day, I realized how badly I wanted to fulfill this dream of being a yoga instructor. I realized that if I wanted this dream fulfilled, I was going to need to carve out my own space. Being the only minority in my training program made me feel some type of way."

This journey of self and community acceptance in the yoga space led Cameo to follow her passion for teaching yoga as a full-time profession, and she divested from the relationship she had with grind culture during the time of her construction career.

In an era when many of us have a sedentary lifestyle due to spending long hours at our computer screens, it's more important than ever to incorporate intentional stretching throughout our workday. Not only can yoga counteract the stiffness of long hours of sitting, but it also increases blood circulation and helps to improve brain function. Yoga can help elevate spirits and mellow tempers, as it has been shown to lower levels of cortisol, the stress hormone, as well as perceived stress in ways likely to foster a more tranquil workplace.

Cameo also speaks to how she's used her yoga practice to transmute anger and promote inner peace within the Black community. "We have a lot of deep-rooted anger and a lot of frustration. Now's the time for us to take back what has been kept from us for thousands of years. Now yoga is being sold back to us and packaged as something different. Before yoga even had poses, it was about meditation. I like to take it back to meditation because that's something that we as the Black community need. We have a lot of anger. We have a lot of depression. We have a lot of PTSD, not just from schools, but from systemic depression, having our brothers and sisters incarcerated. We all know some-body who was incarcerated for weed. We all know some-body who was incarcerated 'just because.' We need to take better care of not just our bodies, but our minds." Cameo sees the importance of yoga as going far beyond exercise, which is great, but it's also a somatic practice that works from within.

Contrary to popular belief, yoga does not always have to be gymnastic in nature. You don't need to have a "yoga body," and it's certainly not a "white people thing." As noted by Cameo, yoga's origins can be found in ancient Egypt through modalities known as Smai Tawi (aka Kemetic yoga), which is a system that combines certain physical movements, controlled breathing, and meditation for healing and revitalization. According to Cameo, "Kemetic yoga and the Smai Tawi yoga are a lot slower. When it became more gymnastics is when European colonizers invaded India. That's when yoga adopted the gymnastics element. That's why I put in a lot of meditation, a lot of slower movement, and people have a hard time with that. But you just gotta ride it. It's a slow roller coaster, but it doesn't mean that you're not moving."

Now's the time for people of the African diaspora to reclaim this ancestral healing modality.

Restorative yoga is an accessible and restful practice that supports you with slowing down and listening to your body by holding poses for an extended period of time. Restorative yoga teaches you how to rest and helps get your body away from a fight-or-flight response. This form of yoga does not require you to exert yourself physically, and you are encouraged to use props, blankets, bolsters, and eye masks in order to enhance comfort.

According to Dr. Gail Parker, "Restorative yoga allows you to come into a deep state of rest without falling asleep, enabling you to notice where the body holds stress and tension and where it is relaxed. This is important because people who are chronically stressed are not always able to identify the difference between tension and relaxation."

One foundational pose in yoga is *Savasana,* a restful pose normally at the end of a yoga practice to let your body reset and recharge. Cameo calls it a rebirth, saying, "Once we go through yoga practice, we're leaving it on the mat. Whatever happened there, whatever you felt, we're leaving it on the mat and we're just gonna surrender . . . to ourselves, to our higher self, and to the earth."

To begin integrating a yoga practice within your workday, start where you are. Even if it's five or ten minutes a day, it matters. It only takes a moment to reclaim yourself. I suggest integrating yoga into your routine three times a week. How might you add some yoga to your current workday? Maybe you take a call off camera and do a legs on the wall pose during the chat. Or you can schedule a ten-minute yoga break right around the time when you get sluggish. For me, that's about four p.m., when my body either needs a nap, a bath, or some physical exertion. Which option I choose depends on my time and capacity for that particular day, but many times I lean on my yoga practice as a part of my thriving tool kit.

Remember, creating a yoga ritual is not about perfection or wearing the perfect yoga outfit; it's about carving out a sacred space for yourself within a chaotic world.

Detoxing from Grind Culture Through the Alchemy of Sound

We use sound for expression, celebration, ceremony, leisure, and healing. Sound therapy has been around since recorded history and is integral to every culture on the planet. Many ancient sites, such as the Egyptian pyramids, were built for sound resonance.

Sound healing is an ancient practice of using sound and vibration as a way to heal the integrated body, mind, and spirit. Western medicine is still catching up to the healing implications of sound healing therapy, though studies show that sound therapy brings brain waves to a slower rhythm and induces state of deep relaxation. Sound healing has significant benefits for treating stress, anxiety, and sleep disorders, as well as reducing cholesterol levels and the risk of heart disease.

Crystal and Tibetan singing bowls in particular support not only relaxation but can bring the body into a state of homeostasis in the face of stress or anxiety. A study published in the *Journal of Evidence-based Integrative Medicine* examined the impact of sound meditation, specifically Tibetan singing bowl meditation, on mood, anxiety, pain, and spiritual well-being. It found participants experienced a significant reduction in tension and a feeling of spiritual well-being also significantly increased through sound healing.

Cymatics is the study of sound and the visual representation of sound waves, as well as their impact on human cells. Simply put, cymatics makes sound visible. Although sound is an invisible force, it shapes our daily lives. Cymatics merges the study of sound, geometry, mathematics, and light to demonstrate the transformative impact that sound can have on the human body and consciousness. The eighteenth-century German physicist Ernst Chladni is famous for studying the physics of sound by playing a sand-topped metal plate with a violin bow to create simple geometric shapes. His work was critical for the future development of cymatics. More than one hundred years later, Hans Jenny started to experiment with different liquids and solids and continuous vibrating frequencies to continue the study of physics and sound. It was Jenny who coined the term cymatics, which contains the Greek word *kyma*, or "wave."

Sound healing can take the form of humming, chanting, mantras, drums, crystal singing bowls, tuning forks, bells, and gongs.

Although I had been exposed to new age spirituality for quite some time, I didn't see myself as someone who could be a sound healer because of the lack of Black representation in the mindfulness and somatics fields. But a few years ago, I delved into research that confirmed the

African origins of sound healing. In the ancient Egyptian temples to promote healing through rest and dreams, there were special resonant sound chambers. Sound was so holy to the ancient Egyptians, they considered all vowel sounds sacred and did not include vowels in written hieroglyphics. Uncovering the origins of this healing modality enabled me to find my place in the world of sound healing and increased my sense of belonging.

During my pregnancy, I was seeking opportunities for deeper, more intentional healing strategies, and I found solace during a sound bath. A sound bath usually consists of lying down in Savasana with a yoga mat, pillows, and an eye mask. During this time you are in a state of deep meditation, listening to sacred instruments like singing bowls, drums, gongs, and chimes.

In my experience, if meditation is taking the stairs, sound healing is taking the elevator. Sound bypasses the thinking part of meditation and drops you into a flow state right away. The chaos of the world recedes, and a sense of well-being takes hold. Sound healing provided the medicine I didn't even realize I was seeking. It tapped into healing past the confines of words and brought me into the realm of embodiment. Sound healing makes you happy in any environment, and I encourage you to incorporate it into your daily life. You can purchase your own singing bowl, attend a live sound bath, or listen to recordings online.

Binaural beats are another method of sound healing that trains your brain to enter states of ease, flow, and focus by playing sounds tuned to a certain frequency. Binaural beats are purported to get the human brain to reach a meditative state at a quicker pace and have been known to reduce anxiety, increase focus and concentration, lower stress, increase relaxation, foster positive moods, promote creativity, and help manage pain.

The Eurocentric approach to the self, work, and health exists in a lineage that began with the ancient Greeks and continues through the Enlightenment thinkers, all of whom saw a clear separation between mind, body, and soul. Scientifically, philosophically, and historically speaking, we seem to be on the verge of reimagining this schism within ourselves. Truly, there is no mind-body separation except in our imaginations—which are very powerful. We have fewer neurons in our brains that we do in the rest of our bodies, notably in the gut. Since the late '60s, the work of evolutionary biologist Lynn Margulis has brought to preeminence the idea that the different parts of single cells were once separate cells that merged together to live in symbiosis. Seen in this light, it is collaboration—not competition—that drives evolution. The individual doesn't really exist. Each of us is a planet, a collection of organisms living and working together.

I think this shift provides a profound opportunity to live into our core values not based on what we say or who we think we are, but rather in our actions and how we show up in our bodies and in our relationships to other bodies. Our current systems have been built around what we believe about the world. Each one of us is trained to think and believe through major institutions including academia, religious groups, popular culture, and our political system. What we think and whose thoughts matter, which gods we worship and what rituals we perform, what beauty looks like and what kind of life we should live—all of this is informed by these institutions. For the most part, our traditional institutions have failed to teach us the art of embodiment. But this dynamic is shifting.

Our old systems are so entrenched that it can be hard to envision any other way. Can we dance our way out of structural inequality? Can we root ourselves in Indigenous ways of knowing to become stewards of the land we thrive on? Can we weave ourselves into being the vast webs of collective care we need? While they might sound fanciful or unfamiliar now, whatever new systems we create will be born out of embodied practices, not just beliefs about the world. Through acts of service, wellness, connection, and memory we will provide for ourselves, our families, our communities, and our earth so that we can be physically, spiritually, and emotionally well, so that we may thrive for generations to come.

Embodiment

Detoxing from grind culture needs the special sauce of embodiment. We can't do this work by reading a book, thinking about it, or meditating from a mind-only space. From within the chaos and pain of the world we have an opportunity to bring forth something new in our bodies. The way forward is not in lectures, ancient tomes, or even political institutions. It is accessible in the simplicity of breath, the divine geometry of sound, the healing rest of yoga. If these things aren't yet in your regular tool kit, I encourage you to try them—although not in a worrying, thinking, or feeling you're not good enough way. Remember Cameo, who didn't think yoga was for her? Or pregnant me, who had no clue that I could be a sound healing practitioner, tapping into the ancient wisdom of my ancestors? If you already do some of these things, what can you do to expand and deepen your somatic practices?

Body Scan Exercise

The body scan is a great relaxation exercise for tuning in to and increasing your ongoing awareness of your body.

For this exercise, you'll want to set aside twenty to thirty minutes in a space where you are least likely to be interrupted. If you have a place where you routinely meditate, that works well. However, unlike in sitting meditation, it's less important in a body scan for you to be sitting up. You can certainly do so if that's more comfortable for you, but for this exercise most prefer to lie down. Just be sure to do so comfortably—a yoga mat or folded blanket can help if necessary. Keep your arms and legs uncrossed and lay in a comfortable but open position on the ground. (If you are familiar with yoga, you might know this as Savasana or Corpse Pose.) Remember that while this is an awareness exercise, it's also for relaxation and the easing of bodily tension. So if you fall asleep, that's actually great!

Begin by closing your eyes and taking three gentle, full breaths. Follow your breath in and out and relax into the idea that this restful observation is all that is required of you right now. If any anxious thoughts arise, simply notice them and then let them go, returning to your breath.

Once you've taken a few breaths, turn your attention to your feet. Notice if you feel any tension or discomfort there. If you do, simply acknowledge it and let it go—there's nothing to be done to change it or work with it. Some find it helpful to imagine silently saying "hello" to any tension or discomfort, followed by a phrase such as "I see you, I understand, I am letting you go." Imagine the tension easing out and your feet relaxing completely. Some people like to imagine that part sinking deeply into the warm and gentle arms of the earth, cradled and safe.

Now move your awareness up to your calves. Notice if you feel any tension or discomfort, and repeat your process of acknowledging it and letting it go.

Continue to move your awareness slowly up into each part of your body—to your knees, your thighs, your pelvis, your stomach, your back—and repeat the process in each area, noticing and acknowledging any tension or discomfort in each part, letting it go, and feeling it release into relaxation and warmth. If there are any parts that seem more tense than others, feel free to spend extra time there, releasing, acknowledging, and allowing yourself to relax into the gentle arms of the planet beneath you.

Once you've moved through your entire body, you may feel deeply relaxed, sleepy, and heavy. Allow yourself to luxuriate in this feeling for as long as you can. Then, when you're ready, slowly open your eyes and gently move your fingers and toes. Take your time and appreciate the way each part of you moves in concert with the other parts. You may want to do some intuitive stretching. Send some gratitude out to your body for all that it does for you. Drink a full glass of water to close out your time.

Mindful Movement

There are a number of movement modalities to explore beyond yoga. I encourage you to try as many as you feel drawn to, but be sure to be aware of any attitudes influenced by grind culture that can sometimes be found even in movement practices that purport to be healing. I'm primarily talking about attitudes and group cultures that promote competition over cooperation and encouragement, pushing one's body past reasonable and healthy boundaries in order to achieve/gain/win and/or incorporate subtle (or at times even not-so-subtle) body shaming. And be aware of these tendencies within as well—grind culture is insidious, and we often carry it with us into many different places.

Here are a couple suggestions for mindful movement you can try.

Walking meditation. Take ten minutes to go on a walk where you focus on being completely in the present moment. At the very beginning of your walk, close your eyes and take some deep breaths. Bring your awareness to your feet and the earth below them. Send some gratitude to your feet and your body for supporting you. And as you walk, see if you can maintain this level of awareness of your body and the world around you. Notice the smell of the air, the feel of the wind on your skin, the warmth of the sunlight. If you find yourself distracted by thoughts of the future or the past, simply bring yourself back to the present by moving your awareness to your feet and their contact with the earth.

Ecstatic dance. If you have the space at home, play some music you love and spend ten to twenty minutes just letting your body move however it wants to. Dancing alone at home may feel weird at first if it's not something you normally do, but try to pay attention to your mood before and after dancing and you may find that even ten minutes spent dancing in your living room has left you in a much brighter, more refreshed place. Alternatively, there may be groups in your area devoted to ecstatic dance or drum circles.

Sound Healing Resources

Sound healing is a great healing modality to integrate into your workday in order to combat workplace stress and anxiety. Some simple strategies to incorporate sound healing into your workday you might try are:

- ○ Play binaural beats for focus and productivity when you are engaging in deep work.

- ○ Play recordings of sound baths during your break time for an energetic reset.

- ○ Invest in a Tibetan singing bowl or tuning fork to restore yourself after a stressful meeting or as a ritual to close out your workday.

....

Thriving Affirmation

I make way for flow, movement, and joy throughout my day.

....

Chapter 6

Boundaries—Trusting Your Yes and Your No

Boundaries are the distance at which I
can love you and me simultaneously.
—Prentis Hemphill

In 2021, Kevin Roose wrote an article for the *New York Times* called "Welcome to the YOLO Economy." Here's how it begins:

> Something strange is happening to the exhausted, type-A millennial workers of America. After a year spent hunched over their MacBooks, enduring back-to-back Zooms in between sourdough loaves and Peloton rides, they are flipping the carefully arranged chessboards of their lives and deciding to risk it all. . . . I started hearing these stories this year when several acquaintances announced that they were quitting prestigious and high-paying jobs to pursue risky passion projects.

The COVID-19 pandemic changed the priorities of folks all over the world in terms of considering what matters and what their nonnegotiables are in a professional environment. An increasing number of working professionals are seeking more than just a paycheck; they are looking for autonomy and respect. They are looking for something that's feeling increasingly mythological as time passes: healthy boundaries at work. Many of us are seeking validation outside of what we can produce and would prefer not to live in a reality where coercion and control are the norm. Old paradigm ideologies of hierarchy, control, and exploitation don't have to be how we conduct business. We can do better—and fortunately, many of us are demanding better. We are beginning to believe that another way outside of grind culture is possible.

Grind culture is the collective imagination of white cis males. This is the current paradigm that most of us perpetuate, whether it's on a conscious or subconscious level. If we do not create boundaries around our capacity to produce, we will put our individual and collective health and well-being at risk. An increasing number of us are beginning to understand that grind culture and the variety of oppressions that perpetuate it leave most of us feeling dissatisfied, frustrated, and wanting more. As we lean into new paradigms and create alternative organizing structures, we will need to teach ourselves how to create and hold healthy boundaries. Boundaries affirm our freedom.

This chapter will break down the importance of healthy boundaries with regard to obtaining and maintaining sovereignty and work-life liberation, how to maintain spiritual hygiene, as well as how to implement physical, emotional, and energetic boundaries in your professional life to increase well-being at work and beyond.

From Codependency to Sovereignty

For most of my life I've been a codependent person—someone whose thinking and behavior are organized around another person, process, or substance. Sometimes called "relationship addiction," codependency is an emotional and behavioral condition that impacts your ability to have a healthy, mutually satisfying relationship. For many years, I navigated my work and personal relationships with the understanding that it was my duty to create order out of other people's chaos. Although this trait was helpful to others in the short term, it caused damage to my sense of self-worth. Many codependents place a lower priority on their own needs to support the needs of others. My codependent behavior was about seeking validation and affirmation through the care of others. Not seeing value in myself, I sought it in being a good friend, employee, boss, or daughter.

When I first heard the word *codependence*, I assumed that this relationship dynamic didn't affect me because I've always been an independent person. However, as I soon came to discover, there are two sides to the codependent coin: some codependent people need people to depend on, and other codependents need to feel needed. I fell into the second category, and I got validation and held up a sense of my identity as a helper, connector, facilitator, and worker. The seductive lie of codependency, for me, was that my codependent behaviors made me worthy.

Accepting my codependency was the hardest part. It was so much a part of my relationship dynamics that it felt too scary to try to change. I spent many years thinking of codependence as just a part of my personality, until I took the space and time to renegotiate the relationships that no longer served me. People with codependency are often in relationships that are one-sided, emotionally destructive, and dysfunctional, with a lack of healthy boundaries. These relationships can be with romantic partners, friends, colleagues, or family members.

Acknowledging the problem and then reclaiming the power of your highest self are the first steps in healing from codependency. The next step is understanding, receiving, and implementing healthy boundaries in our work and personal lives. Healthy boundaries helped me to reclaim my peace and remember my right to thrive.

Setting and Maintaining Healthy Boundaries

Healthy boundaries help us get free from grind culture habits too. Many folks are immersed in grind culture, engaging in too many meetings, working for long periods of time with no breaks, and feeling guilty for resting. All of these symptoms reflect a lack of healthy professional boundaries. Having healthy boundaries is crucial, and here's why:

○ *Healthy boundaries define your identity.* They help you understand and assert what you like and what you don't like. They show others how to respect your preferences.

○ *Healthy boundaries protect your time.* They help you save time for yourself so you can pour back into you. As the saying goes, "You can't pour from an empty cup."

○ *Healthy boundaries bring order.* They offer clarity around job responsibilities, workload, time commitment and capacity, as well as firm start and end times.

○ *Healthy boundaries cultivate respect.* When you define yourself for yourself, you are able to model for others what acceptable treatment looks like with you in daily interactions. When you respect your time, then others will be more likely to respect it as well.

○ *Healthy boundaries preserve your purpose and mission.* When you have healthy boundaries, you reclaim your time and find ways to refuel and restore your spirit. Boundaries make your purpose and mission sustainable over the long term.

Healthy Boundary Practices

Following are some of the practices that I adopted to assert healthy boundaries at work.

I checked in with my personal boundaries. I got really clear on what my preferences were and what conditions were the most affirming and uplifting to my spirit. You are allowed to articulate your needs and wants at work.

I communicated assertively. I stopped apologizing when I was unavailable. I replaced phrases like "Sorry for the delay!" to "I appreciate your patience." I stopped making myself so willing to please and refocused my priority on being respected as opposed to being well-liked. Eek! This was a hard one.

I created structures of transparency. I made sure to get clear details on when I was expected to work, as well as what was and was not in my job description. I ensured that my team worked toward a tracking system that measured the time and capacity of my staff for equitable division of labor.

I delegated work when it made sense. Instead of immediately rushing to pick up extra work so I could look like the ultimate team player, I started to delegate the work in ways that were equitable without it falling on me to pick up the additional labor. When that wasn't possible, I paid to outsource the work in order to reclaim my time.

I owned my yes and my no. I used to be a yes-person. I would be the classic overscheduler. I would say yes when people presented opportunities to me because they sounded nice. I said yes without measuring my time and capacity. Sometimes, this meant that a yes later turned into a no, or an "oops, I can't." Now I say no to a lot more opportunities to make way for the yeses so I can dive deep into purpose and passion. Sometimes circumstances still change and I can't follow through on a yes, but I no longer have to feel guilty about it because I own my yes and my no.

Setting and holding boundaries are not easy. Sometimes doing this will expose a problem or reveal a difficult truth about a relationship or an organization. Very likely, someone will not like what you are saying. You might be implicitly pointing out a failure or oversight on their part. You might get blamed for making a boundary, just as Makiah was written up for using the bathroom during her pregnancy—a simple boundary stemming from her basic human rights.

Boundaries require that we meet reality on reality's terms. We are not superhuman. We cannot save a company, a failing project, or another person. If you are harming yourself to solve a problem that was cocreated at work, you are actually contributing to that problem by hiding how bad it is. If you work all weekend so that an event goes well, no one has to own that the system set up to do events is failing. It's like a form of denial. When we set a boundary that we know could lead to things falling apart, remember: this is brave, vulnerable, and terrifying. You were not granted this one wild and beautiful life to save and prop up everything by yourself.

A Note about Self-Love

Once I understood my own maladaptive relationship patterns, I had to completely shift the way I approached relationships with family, loved ones, and coworkers. I needed to establish healthy boundaries. Boundaries can also fall into the seven categories of rest from chapter 4: physical, mental, emotional, spiritual, social, sensory, and creative.

The boundaries that I particularly focused on at first were physical, emotional, and spiritual. I needed physical boundaries to spend some time in solitude and get reacquainted with myself. I had to check in with myself and ask, *Who was I when I didn't need to be needed? Who was I when*

I wasn't a mother, a wife, a colleague, a boss, or a friend? Who am I at my essence?

To find out, I started courting myself. I initiated my self-love journey around the summer solstice and gave myself a rose petal flower bath infused with sensual herbs and oils like patchouli, lavender, and rose. And while I was in the bathtub, I wrote self-love affirmations to myself and then wrote about all of the aspects of my life I was grateful for. I was completely devoted to pouring love and adoration into myself, and it felt like a new beginning. Once I started living my life as someone who is worthy and deserving of complete care and attention, my world shifted.

You can do this too. Self-love rituals like this one will help you to develop the courage and strength to set healthy boundaries with friends and loved ones. It all starts with self-love. You are the sovereign ruler of your destiny, and you need to show up for yourself fully before showing up for others. Self-love can help you set boundaries even when the people pleaser in you feels guilty for letting others down. Self-love helps you to embrace choosing yourself.

Enforcing Energetic Boundaries

After I activated my courage and power through self-love, I improved my spiritual hygiene and stepped up my energetic boundaries. Spiritual hygiene is the practice of taking care of your energetic body and listening to your higher self. Having strong energetic boundaries is especially important for empaths. Empaths have the ability to sense the energies of people and/or plants and animals, and they tend to take on the emotional states of others—often without realizing it.

There are many empaths currently on this planet. I am definitely an empath, and if you have struggled to protect your energy from becoming enmeshed in the problems of others at the expense of your well-being, you may be one too. Do you always care for others before caring for yourself? As empaths, it's in our nature to want to help others, but our urge to help can be so strong that it can lead us to neglect our personal well-being. Our health is our wealth. Reclaiming our right to wellness as we detox from grind culture means being able to protect our energy as empaths so we can instead focus it on living our authentic truths and, in turn, inspiring the awakening of many other individuals all over the world.

When we don't or can't protect our energy, we can eventually fall into maladaptive ailments like depression, anxiety, and codependency. This can leave us even more susceptible to energy vampires—people who either intentionally or unintentionally drain your energy—and the cycle continues. Unfortunately, in some professional situations we may encounter these individuals on a regular basis. A great way to assert and maintain your energetic boundaries when dealing with an energy vampire is through the following bubble visualization technique.

Bubble Visualization Technique

If you need to attend a meeting with an energy vampire, narcissist, or otherwise unpleasant person, consider using this technique. Before entering or logging on to a meeting, take a deep breath. Ground yourself by checking in with the places where your body connects to the earth under your feet and the pressure where your back and seat connect to the chair or floor. Imagine you are surrounded by an iridescent holographic bubble of spiritual protection. Affirm the following three times: "I AM a sacred and sovereign being." Let your heart swell with self-love and respect, and proceed.

Back when I was in a toxic work environment, I would start each meeting with a grounding meditation and end meetings in gratitude as a way to reclaim my sacredness throughout my workday. When I made the leadership decision to center mindfulness during staff meetings, I helped to facilitate relationship building and camaraderie among my staff by finding ways to flip the narrative of traditional work culture by taking moments of intentional, sacred pause throughout the workday.

Another thriving strategy available to empaths or anyone dealing with a difficult person at work is to take as many opportunities as possible to ground in nature and work outside. This includes taking walking meetings during which you can add sensory rest by going off camera. Can you take work calls on a patio or in a backyard and soak up some vitamin D? In order to engage in these thriving practices and support your grind culture detox on a consistent basis, you'll have to get comfortable with setting healthy boundaries with yourself and others. Empaths are so used to giving, and there's a part of us that loves it, but it's also important to pour that same love back into ourselves as well. Sometimes it helps to imagine yourself as a child you love deeply. You certainly would go to bat for that kid. Alternatively, you can think of supporting future you. Tomorrow, you'll be very grateful for setting that boundary and taking a little extra time and energy for yourself.

Reclaiming Yourself from Workplace Stress

Nakia Dillard is the founder of Magnetic Woman Coach, the culmination of a more than eighteen-year career impacting the lives of others through her service in public health, youth development, and social and food justice work. She holds a Bachelor of Science in community-based health education. Her services as a coach and mentor have impacted the lives of many women and girls.

Nakia's sole mission with Magnetic Woman Coach is to help Black women honor their self-care and leap into their divine calling so that they can experience more joy, fulfillment, and self-love. She supports Black women in putting themselves first, being bold and courageous, and prepares them for their next chapter in life.

Prioritizing healthy boundaries is at the top of Nakia's list for herself and her clients. She discusses the personal struggles she's come up against while working to incorporate healthy boundaries in the workplace: "It hasn't been easy. I'm someone who has struggled with speaking my voice in certain spaces, and especially when I'm in places where I'm often the only Black woman or the one who was holding a lot of the foundation of the work. Challenging that energy in those spaces hasn't been easy, but it has been a must, because I found that I can't be my authentic self otherwise. As someone who believes in honoring who I am, taking care of myself, and that I don't have to be in this emasculated energy, I can't be Nakia if I don't say, 'Hey, this doesn't work.' I'm not going to accept being dumped on. I realized that in order to honor who I am, wherever I am, unfair power dynamics have to also be spoken about in the workplace in order to interrupt it. I'm not going to be burnt out, cried out and fell out over any job."

Nakia shares a nature walk practice that she engages in after a draining work meeting, where she puts on a self-love playlist and listens while she walks and looks intently at the nature around her. "I just kind of walk in an energy and an intention of gratitude. Even though this job is stressful, what am I grateful for right now? Whether it is within the job, or what I'm looking at in that moment, or other pieces of my life, just bringing it back to a state of gratitude and appreciation that I'm still here, breathing [helps]; there's more to life than this situation or circumstance."

After ten or fifteen minutes of this, Nakia returns to her workspace reset, recharged, and refreshed. Nakia's reset ritual allows healing from a multitude of modalities, including music, movement, nature, and affirmations. You don't have to do a whole complicated ritual to access this kind of powerful restoration and healing in your workday. Nakia reminds us to honor our time. We think we don't have time, but she says, "We've got twenty-four hours in a day. You can at least give yourself ten minutes to unplug and to recharge. We've got to shift that mindset. It's so powerful, just how little time it would take, but how much you would gain."

Nakia often drives to her local marina after a long workday to do a complete reset before starting on her "second shift" and doing work for her coaching business after her nine-to-five job. One day, looking at the water and mesmerized by the waves crashing against the rocks, she received a series of affirmations:

I expect the overflow of abundance.
I place myself in situations where I have
access to the abundance that's already mine.

Watching the waves, she moved her gaze from the thrashing ones that hit the shore and started looking farther out, where she couldn't really make out the waves at all. In that moment, she knew:

> *I can expect that those waves that are way down*
> *there are going to eventually come to where I am.*

This opened up for Nakia the idea that we can all expect beyond what we can see. We can look beyond the chaos of what's immediately in front of us and know that we are "abundant and connected to that same energy." All of these insights washed over her in the course of five or ten minutes as she stood still at the ocean, quiet enough to hear a message that nature was sharing with her in that moment. Nakia inspires me, and I hope you too, to honor yourself.

"It doesn't have to be some big thing," she explains. "The more you do it, the more you will open up the door to honoring yourself on a regular basis. It's a process."

The Art of Refusal

Honoring yourself and prioritizing your needs in the workplace can have a ripple effect. When I chose to leave my nine-to-five as a senior program director at a nonprofit, it led the way for conversations around workload as well as the hierarchical leadership structure that perpetuated grind culture within the organization I was employed at. Ironically, my resignation led to many changes in the organization that would not have happened had I said yes to remaining overworked in my position. My perfectionism and my desire to project that I had my shit together had kept me spinning with the wheels of grind culture. I was personally perpetuating the culture of overwork and overwhelm that had been wearing me down.

This has been a profound recurring theme of my healing journey: taking a stand and acknowledging our individual limitations allows us to not only advocate for our own needs, but also inspire change that ripples out in ways we might have never foreseen.

In her book *How to Do Nothing*, written in response to the attention economy that social media and capitalism have helped foster, Jenny Odell speaks to the Art of Refusal, which is the power of saying no. *No* is the pebble that creates the ripple effect of boundaries. Saying no gives others the courage to enforce their boundaries as well. Sometimes people are waiting for just one person to say no, because then that gives them the strength to assert their boundaries as well. Think of Rosa Parks's iconic "no" that sparked the Montgomery bus boycott. *No* holds a powerful magic.

Asserting and enforcing boundaries at work take time. Again, perfection is never the goal. Refusal alone can't summon the mental, spiritual, and economic power it will take to divest from grind culture in our current economic system. There are entrenched power dynamics in the workplace that dictate who can say no and who can't. So, while you might not solve the problem of grind culture by setting a boundary at work, the hope is to reduce the harm of workplace stress and trauma for you and others.

Here are some more ways to set healthy boundaries at work:

Start instituting humane calendaring practices. Your calendar should reflect not just what you need to do, but also what you need to thrive. In addition to your appointments, do you use your calendar to keep track of your overall workload and places of decompression within your day? Be sure to account for administrative time, time to stretch, time to sleep, and time to take care of your wellness needs. The same goes for your to-do list. We often don't include self-care as something we have to do, but that doesn't mean it shouldn't have the same priority as some of the other items on your list that "must" get done. Don't feel guilty about scheduling some time for yourself.

Pull up your calendar for this week. In what ways is your calendar humane? In what ways is it inhumane? Unpack and reflect.

Some tips for integrating humane calendaring practices into your workday include the following:

○ *Be realistic about your capacity.* Are you including time for basic needs, meals, school pickups, shopping and cooking, etc.?

○ *Ask yourself where you can do less.* Are you always doing more out of fear, avoidance, or habit? Interrogate that tendency.

○ *Make space for processing and contemplation.* Solutions to some of the trickiest problems or insights about the next great idea often come to us when we're relaxing, resting, hanging with friends, hiking, playing a game, etc.

○ *Calendar time for thriving!* If you have to schedule a daily bath to get it done, then pencil it in.

○ *Create opportunities for deep work.* Make space at least once or twice a week in order to map out and research creative big-picture ideas and projects.

○ *Block social media.* To support facilitating deep work, as well as sensory rest, consider downloading a time-saving app to reduce your social media time for portions of the day. My go-to app is called Freedom.

○ *Transform your to-do lists into to-thrive lists.* In order to divest from grind culture, we need to stop only prioritizing our to-do lists. It's also about understanding what we need to thrive. This helps to facilitate work-life liberation as well. A sample to-thrive list might look like this:

   • Catch up on email

   • Write ten pages

   • Take a salt bath

- Update student rosters

- Take a walk

Consider your day tomorrow. What do you need to produce and what do you need to thrive then? Write them all down and then try combining the lists.

Find alternate ways to say no. The codependent or perfectionist tendency is to overexplain and apologize when you need to say no. Try to practice saying no with only a short phrase of explanation if needed:

○ I wish there were two of me.

○ I'm not qualified to do that task.

○ I know you will do a great job yourself.

○ I'm not available now, but we can schedule some time later?

○ I can recommend someone who can help you.

Additionally, you can say yes with the terms of your boundary built in with a "yes, but" or a "yes, and":

○ Yes, but I won't be able to start until (date or time).

○ Yes, and I will need the following support to make it happen.

Journal Reflection

Consider your top values in life for a moment, or the things you aspire to. For me, values such as joy, peace, friendship, and honesty come to mind. When it comes to each of these values, write three to five examples for each question of what the highest expression of honoring these values would look like in your work environment and/or life in general. Here's an example:

Value: Joy

What I prefer:

○ Time to play and discover new things I love to do

○ Spending time in nature

○ Warm baths and afternoon naps

What I allow but don't prefer:

○ Boring meetings

○ Scrubbing the toilets

○ Being on camera for meetings

What I don't allow:

○ Humorless work environments

○ Disrespectful or demeaning personal relationships

○ Endless exhaustion and stimulation

Take a look at this list—does it reflect your current daily reality? What are you allowing right now that messes with your most cherished values? Think of one way you can bring boundaries into your life this week that will support your values. It can be just one. This is a lifelong process.

....

Thriving Affirmation

Healthy boundaries help me to give in a way that is authentic and beneficial to my emotional and physical well-being. They build trust within myself and with others.

....

Chapter 7

Allowing Nature to Nurture Us

Knowing that you love the earth changes you, activates you to defend and protect and celebrate. But when you feel that the earth loves you in return, that feeling transforms the relationship from a one-way street into a sacred bond.

—Robin Wall Kimmerer, *Braiding Sweetgrass*

When I was sixteen, I took a road trip with my mother and a couple of her friends up Highway 1 from Los Angeles to Santa Cruz. The Central Coast of California provides staggering views, oceans teeming with kelp forests and wildlife, and mossy primordial redwood groves. Before this, my nature experience had been in city parks, playgrounds, and open spaces on a few field trip excursions. Being a nature buff wasn't a priority or a family value and hadn't been for several generations.

It was my first time visiting Northern California, and I fell in love. In Santa Cruz, we visited a natural agriculture farm, and I tasted the best strawberry of my life. Its sweetness was unlike any other strawberry I had ever had. I came to know that it was not only organic, but also planted and harvested with spiritual intention. It was a revelation to me that I could taste this intention.

On this same visit, I hugged a tree for the first time—a redwood. I felt a vibration of love pulsate out of that tree. The experience forever changed me and my relationship with nature. In the exchange of energy between me and the tree, I understood that my body exists in a symbiotic relationship with nature. I woke up to the ancient knowledge that my well-being was intertwined with the health and well-being of the natural life around me.

Despite this awakening to the power of nature I experienced on this trip, I got lost in school, and then work, and I forgot about the importance of being outdoors. It wasn't until I became an adult, moved to Oakland, and began recognizing the destructive force of grind culture that I started having meaningful experiences with nature again. Now, being in and exploring nature have become an essential tool in my thriving tool kit, one I would no more do without than air, food, or water. Whenever I feel like I'm getting caught back up in grind culture, I know that I can restore and ground myself in the forest, by the sea, or in the mountains.

One of the things that attracted me to living in Northern California is the diversity of natural landscapes and the ability to visit the redwoods or a body of water in under an hour. Access to natural spaces has become increasingly imperative for me.

Nature reminds us to slow down. It invites our awareness and our presence. Being in nature provides a source of strength and regeneration and keeps us in the present moment, where we can set aside dwelling on the past or worrying about the future. Nature holds us, reminds us of the smallness of human problems, and gently reassures us that this too shall pass.

Our Lost Connection to Nature

Americans are detached from the natural world. According to a study sponsored by the Environmental Protection Agency, the average American spends 93 percent of his or her time indoors. We are living in an era of nature deprivation. Nature deprivation has been associated with depression, loss of empathy, and lack of altruism. A 2011 study published in the *Journal of the American College of Cardiology* concluded that time in front of a screen was associated with a higher risk of death. Additionally, their report found that less than 20 percent of Americans participated in outdoor recreation activities like hiking, fishing, kayaking, and camping, and of the people who said they regularly went outside, 63 percent only go outside within ten miles of their homes. It's likely that if you aren't used to walking around your neighborhood, you're even less likely to walk around places beyond your neighborhood, such as parks or nature preserves. And yet having consistent access to natural spaces and activities in nature provides a variety of benefits:

- Lower blood pressure

- Reduced levels of stress and anxiety

- Pain relief

- Improved mood

- Improved physical health

A study conducted by the European Centre for Environment & Human Health at the University of Exeter found that people who spent two hours a week in parks or other natural spaces—either all at one time or spaced over several visits—were considerably more likely to report good health and psychological well-being than those who didn't. Two hours was the absolute minimum for a positive health impact to be documented within the study. This chapter will explore the importance of incorporating nature and plant allies into your daily practice of detoxing from grind culture. We'll take a look at the socioeconomic barriers you might encounter during this process as well as practical strategies to strengthen your relationship with plants and nature.

Forest Bathing

Forest bathing, or *shinrin-yoku*, is a practice that was developed in the 1950s in Japan and consists of taking in the natural atmosphere of a forest. Forest bathing can be as simple as taking a walk in the woods without your phone to connect with nature and to cancel out the noise of the world. It's amazing how quickly a forest can teach you to tap into expanded awareness. Being in this full-sensory symphony increases your health and well-being, so much so that the Japanese government turned this into a national practice to reinforce the positive health experiences associated with these mindful moments in nature. The Japanese are known to have some of the highest life expectancies on the planet, and this nature-based practice is a contributing factor.

The practice of shinrin-yoku consists of taking a walk in nature either by yourself or with a nature guide. When engaging in a forest bath, the focus is not on fitness and increasing your heart rate, but rather on mindfulness and increasing your mental and spiritual health. However, the benefits of this practice can be felt by the physical body as well.

What's more, forest bathing helps people cultivate their sense of smell, which can have positive impacts at the cellular level. David and Austin Perlmutter, a father-son team of medical doctors who research the brain, write in their book *Brain Wash: Detox Your Mind for Clearer Thinking, Deeper Relationships, and Lasting Happiness*, "The mere sniff of a certain scent can shift brain waves and activity from those associated with disease and cognitive decline to those linked with health and wellness." They explain that part of the reason natural aromas quickly calm our nervous system is that smells can cross the blood-brain barrier. These sensations are so powerful that you can probably call up the memory of the smell of a forest by just reading about it—that loamy sweetness is the smell of regenerative life itself.

In addition to the general benefits of being in nature, the research around forest bathing shows many other health benefits:

- Better sleep

- Increased mindfulness

- More energy

- Improved focus

- Boosted immune system

- Faster recovery from illness and injury

The Perlmutters continue, "Nature ultimately rewires the brain for peaceful well-being, and supports the body's overall physiology. It is clear that we need nature to thrive." And yet significant barriers to access exist. Let's look at some of those barriers, and how to overcome them.

The Racial Divide of Green Space

From a very young age, I knew I wanted to move to Oakland, California. Although I grew up mostly in Southern California, I felt this gravitational pull to Oakland. There was a vibe in the city, a feeling of unapologetic Blackness, rich cultural history, and it overall felt like a chill place that was reimagining what a socially just society could be.

Outside of the history and legacy of the Black Panthers that spurred from Oakland, I was also attracted to the city's work, practice, and research around restorative justice approaches in lieu of punitive punishment when conflict arose in schools and communities. Additionally, I had an immense amount of respect for the community gardening and food justice initiatives that were popping up around the city and being used as a teaching tool for the rest of the country to learn from and operationalize. Oakland held within it the essence of a city that felt like home.

In spring 2020, I was living in East Oakland with my husband and our one-year-old son. Three years earlier, we had purchased a house on a notoriously dangerous street corner. It was our family's first home, and in many ways being able to own this home in an increasingly gentrified city experiencing a massive housing crisis felt like a huge blessing. We were happy to be first-time homeowners. Most of our neighbors were caring, friendly, and close-knit.

However, the neighborhood was also rife with issues. During our time living in East Oakland, I witnessed two shootings, saw outbursts of domestic violence in the middle of the street, and lived across from an abandoned house turned crack den. Meanwhile, the park closest to our home was the most underresourced in the city. After getting accosted while walking by myself, most times I didn't feel safe alone outside.

In order to get quality outdoors time, I drove into the Oakland Hills to regional parks like Roberts Regional Recreation Area and Leona Canyon Regional Open Space Preserve, which fortunately were only about a fifteen-minute drive away. The COVID-19 pandemic meant we had to stay home or in our neighborhoods. This was disheartening and detrimental for people who lived without access to abundant safe green space.

Right before the pandemic hit, my husband and I had made the difficult decision to put our house on the market. As our little one was getting older, we didn't want him to think the violence in our neighborhood was normal. We wanted to walk him to parks safely and to not be afraid of what he might witness as outside our front door.

Once the riots broke out as a result of George Floyd's murder, it became abundantly clear that we had made the right choice. On the last night that we stayed in our East Oakland home, it felt like a war zone, with a mixture of gunshots and fireworks coming from every direction. Years of systematic disenfranchisement echoed in these thunderous sounds.

That same night, I gathered a couple friends to perform a neighborhood cleanse. We lit a bonfire in my cement backyard and smudged herbs like yarrow, sage, and palo santo; sprinkled Florida water; and released prayers and good intentions for the neighborhood and its residents. In this way, we paid our respects to the neighborhood as we embarked on a new housing journey. It was sad to leave on such a violent note, but we were clear that the neighborhood could no longer sustain our family's ability to thrive due to the impact of environmental racism and redlining.

The Impact of Environmental Racism and Redlining

Environmental racism is a form of systemic oppression wherein communities of color are disproportionately impacted by environmental toxins. Whether it's lead pipes, a lack of infrastructure, food deserts, degraded soil, or policies that force POC to live in close proximity to toxic waste, environmental racism leads to greater health problems. In 2007, Dr. Robert Bullard, known as "the father of environmental justice," produced research that African American children were five times more likely to have lead poisoning from proximity to waste than white children. Furthermore, his research found that Black Americans making $50,000 to $60,000 a year were more likely to live in polluted areas than their white counterparts making $10,000. This is a staggering finding. Additionally, Bullard's work links the impact of environmental racism with climate change. His research affirms that the negative impact of climate change is felt earlier and more acutely in countries and cities that have more people of color.

East Oakland has the highest concentration of Black residents in Northern California, as well as a large Latinx population. A study done by the Federal Reserve Bank of

San Francisco found that East Oakland residents had significantly higher rates of asthma, diabetes, obesity, mental disorders, emergency room visits, assaults, and teen births. This inequity stems from a long history of racial inequality, which has led to reduced economic opportunities, with over 48 percent of the population living under the poverty line.

As discussed earlier in this book, redlining is the systematic denial of services to residents of racially associated neighborhoods or communities, either explicitly in laws or lending policies, or through raising the prices of real estate. Once my family and I moved to Walnut Creek, a wealthy suburb about twenty minutes outside of Oakland, the long-term effects of redlining were impossible to miss. Walnut Creek was so abundant and resourced, it almost felt wrong. In East Oakland, the only grocery store within walking distance had been a corner store with limited supplies at high prices. In Walnut Creek, retail shops, public green space, and grocery stores and eateries were abundant—and yet somehow food and gas prices were cheaper than in the impoverished neighborhood we had just moved from. Research has proven that the poor actually pay more for basic goods than the wealthy.

It probably won't surprise you that the racial breakdown of Walnut Creek is 78 percent white and 0.2 percent Black. This is common when it comes to neighborhood design in US cities. According to an opinion piece written by Sheryll Cashin for Politico, "Anti-Black habits of disinvestment and plunder continue to this day. Government at all levels overinvests in affluent white space and disinvests in Black neighborhoods, with the exception of excessive spending on policing and incarceration."

In our new neighborhood, pedestrian highways wove through the whole city, attached to hiking trails, parks, and open spaces. We were sandwiched between two botanical gardens, a state-of-the-art playground that looked like it would require an admission fee, as well as access to a lake and a pond. For the first time in years, my family could walk outside our home straight into green space. Although I immediately missed being around people of color and Oakland's cultural ties, I noticed a rapid improvement in my physical and mental health. Connection to nature was key.

Green Space on the Road

My husband and I thought we would be much older when we fulfilled this particular dream, but after selling our home we purchased an RV instead of investing in a stationary home. Wanting more nature in our lives and time to connect in the open air as a family surpassed our desire to own land.

We both put in for time off work and managed to take the longest vacation I had taken in years: three weeks total with seventeen days on the road. We had a nightly ritual of watching the stars and took some amazing walks and hikes together, all over the country. I grew up very low income and didn't know anyone who vacationed with an RV, so it was a surreal experience for me. Early on, we let go of rigid expectations about covering a certain number of miles and decided we wanted to enjoy the actual experience of seeing the great outdoors. It was a true vacation, not a race against the clock that felt like an extension of grind culture.

When we gave ourselves the gift of time, we were able to make it up as we went along. I loved the feeling of waking up in a warm bed surrounded by trees. Each morning, I felt more rested than the one before. My nervous system fell in line with nature's rhythms.

Outside of quality time with family and star-filled nights, some of my favorite parts of the trip were the sound healings I was able to perform at natural sacred sites around the United States. In Canyonlands National Park in Utah, and at Dinosaur National Monument in Colorado, I was able to connect with the earth in a special way with the power of stillness and sound.

Systemic Racism in Natural Spaces

In order to take this trip, I had to overcome some fears and limiting beliefs, most notably my fear of traveling as a Black family.

Amanda Machado wrote in a recent *Sierra Club* magazine article about how, in her lectures, she reminds the outdoor community of the history of many of its beloved places:

I remind my white-dominated audiences that the outdoorsy state of Oregon was the only state to write the exclusion of Black people directly into its constitution and that in the 1920s the state had the largest Ku Klux Klan organization west of the Mississippi River. I remind them that the states most known for their beautiful outdoor areas—like Montana and Idaho—also report the highest rates of hate crimes. I tell them about the swastikas carved on rock-climbing boulders in Colorado and the racist names of rock-climbing routes that the community has never renamed. I tell them that, when I was growing up in Florida, I could not visit any state park without first passing through a row of Confederate flags draped in front of almost every house leading up to it.

I too had a lot of anxiety around how my family would be perceived in places like Wyoming, Utah, and Idaho. The summer of 2020 was racially tense, with the presidential election looming. We did not know how traveling in red states would go. As we started our road trip, I felt panicked as I sat with the racial implications of what we were doing. How dangerous was this idea? We had no friends who were doing what we were doing, traveling cross-country via RV. We kind of felt like weirdos. Fortunately, our family had a very welcoming experience during our time on the road.

We definitely stuck out as the only Black family in a lot of the places that we visited, but folks were supernice.

We all need to incorporate nature retreats into our lives. People of color have the same privilege and right to see our nation's remotest lands as anyone, and yet in countless conversations with POC, I've heard nature-based activities described as "a white people thing." This is by design. Nature gives so many benefits, and like so many other valuable resources, the most elite groups in our society have the most access to it. Grind culture and racism deprive people of color of the affordable, powerful healing of parks, waterways, and green spaces. According to Outdoor Industry's 2019 Outdoor Participation Report, African Americans were the ethnic group least likely to visit federal lands. Additionally, a report conducted by the Hispanic Access Foundation and the Center for American Progress found that "communities of color are almost three times more likely than white communities to live in 'nature deprived' areas, those that have less or no access to parks, paths, and green spaces."

Breaking this cycle starts with us. Organizations like Outdoor Afro and GirlTrek are working to increase the visibility of people of color occupying green spaces. Outdoor Afro is leading the charge with cultivating places for Black people to meet up and engage in nature-based activities all across the United States. Meanwhile, GirlTrek combines civil rights education and history and walking campaigns that support physical and emotional health and well-being. Both of these organizations and many local ones are doing great work with turning the tide with Black people reclaiming green spaces. A simple Google or Meetup search might open up a whole new world for you and your family.

Integrating Nature into Your Professional Life

You might be wondering how you can find time to integrate nature into your daily life, especially if it's not geographically close to you. One way to get more nature into your life is to integrate it into your workday. Consider scheduling time for one walking meeting or phone call per day. If it's not logistically possible or safe to walk outside and meet, look for a place to work with access to sunlight. Consider taking a daily vitamin D supplement to support, not getting enough sunlight due to lack of outdoors time. Another way to integrate nature into your life if you must be indoors all day is to play a naturescape on YouTube. Remember how the smell of the forest was easy to imagine? Listen to sounds of ocean waves, forests, waterfalls, or birdsong and do some creative visualization to connect to nature.

One practice that I like to integrate is keeping a lot of space on Fridays for grounding in nature. Fridays are my days to decompress and tap into my creative potential. I make sure to keep my schedule light so that I can visit local parks or go on hiking excursions. I use this time to plan and reflect for the upcoming week as well as to reflect on lessons learned. If I have to book an appointment on a Friday, I exclusively book phone appointments to give my eyes a screen break. Work doesn't have to be stressful. You can invite ease and flow into your workday with the assistance of nature and its allies.

Using Plant Allies

Once we begin to reconnect with nature and we tap into the earth element, our universe expands and we discover that there are allies all around us. Part of our task when we detox from grind culture is remembering and reclaiming the ancestral knowledge and wisdom of African and Indigenous peoples. Before capitalism and colonization existed, humans shared an intimate relationship with the land, which provided food, shelter, and medicine. Plant allies provide an instructional template from the natural world to support reconnecting with our ancestors as well as the wisdom of the earth. Plant allies can be accessed in a variety of ways: teas, tinctures, nutrition, aromatherapy, gardening, and more. In this section, we'll discuss how to integrate plants and the natural life into your daily routine in accessible ways.

Emilyn Sosa is a Black Dominican and femme-identified herbalist who lives with her extended family in New York City. Her wellness enterprise, Folk Mondays, is an herbal line of support to increase wellness among individuals at work. Emilyn's passion around plants and herbs has been a necessary tool for helping her cope with the traumas she endured in her own work life. After running up the corporate ladder into her late twenties, she reached a point where she realized that her job didn't care about her as a person. "That realization kind of hit hard," she said. "I had focused so much of my energy on trying to produce and trying to prove something to someone else when really I had to take a step back and refocus on myself. That's how I found the work of Sacred Vibes Apothecary in Brooklyn, which led me on my herbalism journey."

Emilyn believes that plant allies can help your nervous system recover from the dysregulating impact of grind culture. She speaks of her relationship with a plant from the Dominican Republic called broad leaf thyme, or *oregano poleo*: "My grandmother gifted me with the oregano poleo plant I have growing in my room, and it's a plant that I go to when I doubt my magic and my relationship with God. Sometimes I can be so hard on myself because I feel like I'm not where I want to be. Sometimes I get caught up in the spiral of thinking I haven't done enough. Working with plant medicine is like returning home." (In addition to being a seasoning for food, thyme has antiseptic abilities and can be used to treat coughs and infections. You can also put it under your pillow for a restful sleep and to prevent nightmares.)

After taking some time to heal herself, Emilyn started working on creating workday rituals and daily practices, along with focusing more on nutrition, to shift her relationship to the workplace for herself and her clients.

For people who are looking to cultivate a deeper relationship with plant allies, Emilyn recommends using tinctures, concentrated herbal extracts that are portable and can be used topically, orally, or added to your favorite beverage. There are tinctures that you can make or that you can purchase depending on your time and capacity.

Another way to utilize plant allies is by incorporating adaptogens into your daily diet. Adaptogens are herbs and mushrooms that adapt to meet the needs of your body and reduce the impact of stressors. They also promote a sense of balance and homeostasis within the immune system. You can take them in teas, powders, or tinctures. Some common adaptogens include the following:

- Lion's mane

- Chaga

- Reishi

- Ashwagandha

- Turkey tail mushrooms

- Ginseng

Emilyn reminds us to start small—subtle changes make a difference. "Sometimes people think, 'Oh well, I'll try to get inspired. So I've got to buy all these things.' But honestly, just like with any habit, you start small and work your way from there."

It should be noted that you don't want to take a bunch of herbs unless you know what they are and how they interact with your body. Ask an expert in natural medicine, Eastern medicine, or herbal medicine. Also keep in mind that plant medicine for your work life is all about what is readily available; so if you're not ready to steep tea with loose herbs, go with a more user-friendly boxed tea. Start where you are.

Taking the time to incorporate herbs into our day helps us to reclaim our sacredness and our connection to nature during our most stressful moments. I love using a rose water mist throughout my workday. It makes me feel beautiful and reminds me that I am worthy of care and attention in those moments when I want to go into my default grinding mode.

If you are curious about diving into the world of plants but are unsure of where to start, consider downloading a plant identification app. Getting to know our plant neighbors grounds us and deepens our connection to our immediate environment. Understanding the role that plant allies play in our world expands our view of the sacredness of the world. Plant allies are a tangible reminder that the universe has our back.

Thriving Practice: Take a Nature Walk

Try taking a nature walk without your cell phone. For an added connection to nature, try earthing: walking barefoot outside. Earthing has many health benefits, including reducing inflammation, improving sleep patterns, and reducing stress. And it couldn't be simpler. Just take off your shoes and socks and spend a little time standing, walking, or resting in nature.

If you want to go on a nature walk but are unable to part from your phone, no sweat. Try listening to an audiobook focused on self-improvement or spiritual development. Consider this your moment of spiritual reset. At some point during your walk, find a tree to meditate under for five or ten minutes. Try to do this without any noise from your phone as you soak in the natural elements.

....

Thriving Affirmation

My relationship with plants mirrors my relationship with myself: expansive and intentional.

....

Chapter 8

The Sacred Workspace

If every moment is sacred, and if you are amazed and
in awe most of the time when you find yourself breathing and not crazy, then you are in a state of constant
thankfulness, worship and humility.
—Bernice Johnson Reagon

I spent a few years working as a professor in child and
adolescent development at San Francisco State University.
During my time there, I decided to curate a nontraditional
workspace for myself. Discarding my idea of what a typi-
cal college professor's office should look like, I tailored my
office to meet my own needs and style choices, filling the
room with bold colors and bohemian print fabrics, cozy
throw pillows, fairy lights, and a vibrant tarot deck. I hung
illustrations and inspirational quotes on the walls.

I made these style choices to promote my own well-
being, but I noticed a positive impact on my students. I
held regular office hours and had an open-door policy for
students. I was there to discuss assignments, but I also supported and case managed students who were first-generation

college students and helped direct them to tutoring, counseling, and financial resources on campus so they could get the most of their college experience and graduate without delays. The warmth and texture that my office provided helped my students to feel welcome and cared for. Sharing snacks or tea there also worked to break down barriers so that I could serve my students more effectively.

My office was an extension of my work and aligned with the legacy that I wanted to leave on the campus and in students' lives. The space nurtured and held me and my work and, in turn, created a nurturing environment in my professional ecosystem.

That office was a sacred workspace for me. For many of us, work is a place we spend most of our waking hours doing things we'd rather not be doing. What would happen if we brought our sacred well-being and our daily work lives just a step closer? In my experience, the results can be profound.

Think of how you feel when you enter a space you love—a cherished family member's kitchen, an art gallery, a religious sanctuary. What do you feel when you walk into a space that is aligned, when its people, design, energy, and mission all seem to sing in harmony? Calm? Energized? Curious? Empowered? These spaces don't have to be fancy—you can just feel the special energy of a place that is practical, embodied, and sacred all at once.

We've spent a lot of this book focused on you—what you feel like, your history, and your habits. Now it's time to expand that awareness into the spaces in which you live and work. Your relationship to your workspace is directly tied to your quality of life, mental health, well-being, and overall productivity. Part of reimagining our relationship to work is to reimagine our office space and center its impact on our well-being. When we take time to cultivate a sacred workspace, we acknowledge our humanity and our right to thrive at work in a small but powerful way. Having a space that makes you feel happy, uplifted, and energized can alleviate work-related trauma and stress. It can also promote a productive work environment by reducing energy drags, boosting your mood, and helping you feel good about focusing on and completing necessary tasks. Cultivating a sacred workspace can tap into the formidable energy of visualization and manifestation. Preparing an abundant, flowing workspace can work to mirror and attract the professional life of your dreams.

This chapter will walk you through some of the basics of creating a sacred workspace, including assessing the strengths and opportunities within your current setup, how to cleanse your workspace and set intentions to get what you need, and how to enhance your work environment using nature's four elements.

Workspace Assessment

Take a moment to reflect on how your workspace is currently structured. Notice how it enhances or takes away from your workflow. Most often, when we think about our workspace, we're thinking of optimizing it for productivity. This assessment looks at more than that and raises the bar. How can your workspace enhance your overall joy and well-being?

To start, look at your current workspace. How does it make you feel? Write at least three sentences to describe the space and any emotions it brings up. For example, maybe your space is cluttered and you feel cooped up. Or maybe your space is full of light, and you feel alert and awake while you're there.

Now single out three of the most undesirable items in your workspace. Name them and say why they feel undesirable. For example, maybe the fluorescent lights give you a headache. Or your books are spread out everywhere, and you can't find what you need.

Next, imagine the workspace of your dreams. Take some time with this one, starting with a minute or two of meditation with your eyes closed. Visualize an ideal workday from start to finish in your space. What do you see? What do you feel? What are you doing?

Let the answers you gave in this assessment be your launching pad for creating a workspace that embodies the professional life of your dreams. If it was easy to zero in on the negative aspects of your space, try to locate the items that take away from your joy and remove or modify them. Start with the things you interact with every day.

Look at your desktop. Maybe you have a pencil cup that's boring, and only half of the writing implements work. Is there another container that you can use to create a more vibrant place to reach for pens and pencils? Can you take five minutes and clear whatever's in there that you don't like or don't use? I have a friend who says you should always invest in a garbage can you love. It may sound silly, but anything you use every day that's ugly or that you don't like will wear your energy on a subliminal level. The details matter. Tending to the details can uplift your overall mood and well-being. One of my favorite ways to do this is with a good space clearing.

Flow and Energy in the Workplace

Ancient spiritual traditions and modern physics agree that matter is made up of energy. When energy is flowing freely, it moves like water with no impediment or stagnation. Our physical spaces are extensions of our bodies. If we are feeling stagnation within our bodies, then this can manifest in our physical space as well. For example, think of a time when you have felt depressed or hopeless. Often, this feeling of disempowerment extends to your physical space as well: dirty dishes and laundry pile up; clutter gathers on surfaces; something in the fridge starts to smell sour. Sometimes the very act of cleansing and clearing can change our emotional state.

Cultures all over the world practice energy work through something called space clearing. Space clearing goes beyond cleaning your room or cleaning off your desk and includes clearing your space of stagnant energy. Stagnant energy can develop when a space is exposed to conversations and thoughts with high amounts of negative thought patterns such as fear, jealousy, hatred, dread, or guilt. In order for work to be joyful, this blocked energy has to be able to flow through and out of your space.

Western belief systems downplay the intrinsic energy, vibration, and consciousness of everything around us. Your computer, your chair, and your floor coverings and windows all have an energy, even a consciousness. These energies contribute to the overall feeling and potency of your space. Additionally, the energies in your space respond to and integrate with your energy and intentions. Before you do a space clearing, it's important to have a specific intention in mind. You might be focused on increased well-being, abundance, creativity, focus, calm, or a myriad of other desires that you want to see fulfilled. Take a moment to pause and think about one or two intentions that would benefit you and your space.

Space clearing can help to reinvigorate your physical and emotional space to promote a spirit of thriving within your workday. It's one thing to clear away the dust and dirt that accumulates over time, as well as clutter and non-useful items in your workspace. These certainly can have a negative impact on your mind as well as your overall peace and well-being. It's another thing to clear toxic energy from your space, which can lead to avoidance, procrastination, flagging energy, and much more. If our bodies, minds, and spirits can be ignored in the name of grinding, then so can our physical spaces.

You might think you're too busy to take the time to clear your space or that it won't have any impact, but in those moments when the work seems the most overwhelming or you are at your wit's end, it makes even more sense to tend to your physical space. What's more, you might be surprised by the outcome of taking this time when you feel you can least afford it. Something as simple as cleaning out a drawer can help you to reprioritize and reclaim thriving. Beautifying your workspace with flowers, fabrics, or artwork is an easy way to infuse moments of joy at work, even if you have negative feelings about your current place of employment or career path. When you tailor your physical workspace toward the life you want to have, you invite major shifts.

Space Clearing Using the Four Elements

The elements of earth, water, air, and fire are important tools for creating a sacred workspace that centers balance, flow, and abundance.

Earth

The earth element grounds us in physical reality and embodied practice. It connects us to nature and to the cycles of seeding, tending, and harvest that provide powerful guiding metaphors for any kind of work we do. The earth also reminds us about what matters and what doesn't.

Here are a few ways to infuse your workspace with the earth element:

- Sound (drumming, crystal singing bowls, rattles)
- Plants
- Crystals

We've already discussed the sacred power of sound healing. Adding a drum, singing bowl, or small speaker to your space can have a huge impact.

Living plants and cut flowers refresh the air and balance the energy of electrical or manufactured items in your space. If you don't have a green thumb, never fear. There are several hardy varieties of houseplants that will do well in whatever lighting and humidity conditions you have. Just be sure to match the plant's needs with where you plan to put it to make sure it's a good fit.

As for crystals, adding a few to your work surface, or slipping them into your pocket, can bring a sense of peace and harmony to your space. I encourage you to seek out a few to see how they make you feel. Crystals are a part of the earth, and they are energetically tuned to different kinds of healing energy. There are a number of reasons given by various crystal experts as to why and how they work (including theories about magnetic energies and color harmonies), but the most important thing in my opinion is that they work for you. You can find a number of books that can help you decide the different crystals you'd like to seek out, and I've listed a few of my favorite types of crystals below that have helped me personally detox from grind culture.

Alternatively, you can use an intuitive approach, especially if there's a crystal and gem shop in your area. This method involves simply visiting a space where there may be a wide range of options and then seeing where you are led. Try to be as open as possible; you may be surprised by what you find. Some people also like to hold their hands over a selection of stones to see if they feel a warmth or tingling in their hands to signal their need for a specific one.

Here is a small list of my favorite go-to crystals for detoxing from grind culture:

- Amazonite: inspires truth, self-love, communication, and integrity; soothes the brain and the nervous system; balances masculine and feminine energies; soothes emotional trauma and alleviates worry and fear

- Aragonite: promotes inner balance, mental clarity, confidence, transformation, and ambition; promotes self-healing; encourages tolerance and flexibility

○ Desert rose selenite: quiets the mind and eases worry and anxiety; increases our sense of self-worth and self-confidence and motivates us to act; highlights subconscious thought patterns and removes blockages related to growth and progress

○ Leopard skin jasper: balances chaotic energies, grounds and stabilizes us, and promotes courage

○ Obsidian: shields against negativity and blocks psychic attacks; brings clarity; helps you to know who you truly are

○ Rose quartz: deepens self-love and infuses loving energy, abundance, and joy into our lives; fosters a deep sense of compassion and care; taps into divine feminine energy to help enhance ease and flow at work

Water

Water represents flow, which is essential for a productive and joyful workspace. Many cultures and healing modalities also associate water with our emotional lives, which so often get blocked or repressed within grind culture. We are mostly made of water, so when we incorporate water throughout our workspace, it can promote a healing and soothing atmosphere.

Here are a few ways to infuse your workspace with the water element:

- A water fountain
- A spray bottle with essential oils and water
- A work bath

A small water fountain that fits on your desk can provide visual and sound stimulation, and it also regulates the humidity in dry spaces. The flow of the water not only is soothing, but it also reminds us to move freely through our work, like water over stones.

Diluted essential oils are great for freshening up a space and just adding a little bit of moisture to the air. Try peppermint and sweet orange when you need to focus. Lavender and ylang-ylang can be wonderful for creating a calm environment. Just be sure to read the labels to ensure your mixture is safe to breathe in (some are known to be irritants), and never apply essential oils directly on the skin.

When you're feeling particularly stressed and overwhelmed, taking a bath in the middle of your workday is a great way to facilitate your grind culture detox process. This is obviously most accessible to people who work from home, but I do have a friend who spends an hour soaking and using the sauna at a traditional Korean bathhouse once a week. Perhaps you could negotiate a work-from-home day a few times a month, during which you can incorporate this ritual.

Since I've taken the steps to incorporate regular baths into my routine, I've noticed greater focus and clarity, fewer aches and pains, softer skin, and an overall deeper sense of peace. If you're able to, I recommend not bringing your work into the tub. But if not working seems impossible, there are still ways to reclaim your peace. Use your bath to check your emails or get some calendaring or reading done. Or you could employ this time to get some answers to questions that have been plaguing you and invite yourself to consider another perspective.

You can add to your bathwater up to a half pound of salt (Epsom salts, Himalayan salt, or Dead Sea salt). Consider also a few drops of essential oils that promote invigoration, like peppermint, eucalyptus, orange, or lemon. Have plenty of drinking water close by to stave off dehydration. And give yourself a good chunk of time—forty-five minutes to an hour—to really take in the healing element of water as you work, think, or plan. Banish any guilt that arises! You are cultivating work-life liberation.

Air

The air element rules the sharing of intellect through communication, clarity, and beauty. Every minute of our waking lives we spend breathing, and the swirling currents and eddies of wind and weather on the planet impact us in ways large and small every single day. We've all experienced times when our lives have felt stagnant or closed in, and the exhaustion that accompanies grind culture can absolutely amplify these issues. In times like these, the element of air can bring insight, clarity, and refreshment.

Here are a few ways to infuse your workspace with the air element:

- An essential oil diffuser
- Incense
- Smudging herbs
- Opening windows and/or running fans
- Breathwork

Diffusing essential oils is similar to the water element method with the spray bottle and diluted oils; both freshen your space with natural oils, but the diffuser hums along consistently in the background. Again, be sure to check the label of whatever oil you're interested in to make sure it won't irritate your lungs and that it's safe for children and pets if they are a part of your household.

I love incense, and keep it around at home and at work to cultivate a good, cozy atmosphere. Try using cinnamon for abundance, patchouli for creativity, or lavender for a sense of calm.

Smudging herbs like sage, palo santo, and sweetgrass are wonderful not just for their scent, but for the promise they offer of wiping a slate clean. Try smudging in between long, tedious meetings and conversations during your workday and notice how the space feels refreshed and renewed. (Note that, depending upon where you plan to smudge, you might need to watch out for smoke alarms.)

It doesn't get very cold in the Bay Area, but even if it did, I would still recommend opening windows and/ or running fans for a short period to circulate the air in your workspace. Running air-conditioning in the summer and heat in the winter can make the indoors seem stale or stuffy; getting some fresh air in from outside will rejuvenate the energy in your space.

Another way to harness the power of air is with breathwork. By taking time out of your day to focus on your breath, you not only give yourself the gift of mindful pauses and breaks, but also a boost of refreshing oxygen, a chance to relax any tense muscles, and a reminder to slow down and be present. There are many different kinds of breathwork, but even one or two very simple breathwork breaks during the day can be helpful.

Here's one simple exercise to try:

Sit up as straight as you can wherever you are in this moment. Close your eyes and gently place your hands on your chest. Breathe in steadily for a count of four. Hold the breath for a count of four. Release your breath slowly for a count of four. Pause for a count of four. Repeat this cycle three or four times.

When you've finished, take note of any sensations in your body. You may feel generally a bit steadier or calmer. If not, that's fine too. These exercises become more powerful the more you do them.

Fire

Fire is the element that initiates ideas through action, passion, creativity, and quick reflexes and that metaphorically burns away what no longer serves us. All elements are cleansing in their own way, but fire has a dramatic presence that can leave a space feeling bright and clean.

Here are a few ways to infuse your workspace with the fire element:

- Candles

- Smudging herbs or incense

- Good lighting (both natural light and filtered or incandescent bulbs)

Candles are a classic way to bring the fire element into your workspace—and there are so many versions to choose from. The candle's color may have some significance, too: try green for abundance, blue for clear thinking and communication, or yellow for positive energy.

Air activities like smudging and incense are also related to fire. See my notes in the air section above for suggestions on specific types to try.

Our sun is a constant fiery presence in our lives, and we benefit in ways both emotional and physical when we spend mindful time in direct sunlight. Since we spend so much time at work, you'll want to make sure your lighting there is as good as it can be. Consider the light sources in your space—does the quality of the light help or hinder your mood and energy? If you have access to natural light, use mirrors to reflect that light and heat into your space from the life-giving sun. If you don't have natural light, structure time in your day to get outside as often as you can. Also, some people do better with filtered light bulbs or incandescent light sources indoors.

....

Fire Purification Ritual

Fire is a great purifier, and we are becoming increasingly aware of its importance to the planet—for example, in maintaining the delicate balance of forest ecosystems. One way to engage the cleansing effect of fire in your life is to enact a small fire purification ritual. (If you have access to a firepit or fireplace, this is ideal; but if not, you can perform a version of this ritual with a candle and a fireproof bowl.)

First, write down some habits, issues, actions, feelings, perspectives, or situations you'd like to move out of your life.

When you're done, choose three from the list and write them on small slips of paper. Then burn each slip of paper in your fire source. If you want to add other ritual elements, such as music or incense, definitely do so. As the paper burns, visualize what your life might be like without those attitudes, actions, or feelings. If prayer or meditation is a part of your practice, this would be a great time for this as well.

....

Sacred Workspace Cleanse

This cleanse will help you remove any heavy, stagnant, or unwanted energies from your workspace and clear the air in both a physical and spiritual sense. It will also help you attract more focus, relaxation, and flow, as well as create a space that is pleasing to your mind, body. and spirit. Feel free to adapt any part of this ritual to your own needs and preferences.

You will need:

○ A smudge stick (try sage, palo santo, or cedar)

○ Incense

To start, clean your space with traditional cleaning products (organic products are preferred). Make sure dust and cobwebs are removed, floors are swept or vacuumed, and surfaces are wiped clean.

Take inventory of any items in your space that aren't being used and don't bring a sense of joy. If you can remove these things entirely, do so! If you can't, temporarily remove them from your space during the cleanse.

Open all the windows and doors. Then light your smudge stick and set your intentions to clear all energies that no longer serve you. Walk around and use the smoke almost like a paintbrush, gently and methodically sweeping it throughout your space. Make sure to focus on the corners—energy spirals in a circular motion, and stagnant energy can get stuck there. Also focus on any areas where you hide things away, like a drawer, closet, or file cabinet. Clear the space of any items that are no longer needed and smudge this space as well. During this process, take time to invite any energy that no longer serves you to exit through the open windows and doors, allowing new energy to flow in.

Once you've smudged all areas of your workspace, close your windows and doors. Then light your incense, taking a moment to set an intention for what you would like to invite into your space. (The incense that you choose should be a pleasing, grounding fragrance for you. Some of my favorite blends include frankincense, patchouli, and cinnamon.) This last step is very important. If you cleanse your space but don't call in what you want, the old energy will resettle and you won't get the full benefits of the cleanse. If you don't know what you want, consider inviting in purpose, passion, or new inspiration.

Complete this cleanse as often as you are intuitively guided to do it.

Furnishing Your Sacred Workspace

Ultimately, you are the authority on what feels best for your workspace. You'll know which items make you feel comfortable, happy, and productive and which ones just feel like clutter. You'll also know how you want to have things arranged and how you want to present your space to others. Here are a few final ideas of things you might want to incorporate as you're putting the finishing touches on your space:

- A yoga mat for stretching

- An outdoor workspace option

- Space for collaboration and privacy

- Full-spectrum light bulbs, multiple light sources

- Photos and artwork that bring you joy

- Cozy comforts such as pillows, beanbag chairs, or floor cushions

- Fidget cubes or puzzles

- A balance ball or balance disk

- Ergonomic furniture

- Herbal teas and tinctures

- Heating or cooling pads

- Air and water filters

- A standing desk

- A good-quality speaker

- Coffee-table books, art books, poetry compilations, or albums and a record player

Setting Workspace Intentions

All creation begins with intention. Each day, prior to starting your workday, begin with an intention for what you would like to manifest that day. This can be done through journaling, meditating five minutes prior to your workday, or even practicing a quick yoga stretch. The way you set your intentions is up to you—the important thing is that you do it and remain consistent.

A fun way to set and keep your intentions incorporates the plants in your home. Select a houseplant that needs to be watered once or twice a week. Set one to three intentions you want to manifest for your work and write them on small slips of paper. For example, you might write, "I am abundant" or "I attract resources effortlessly." Fold up the notes as small as you can, and bury them in the soil of the plant. Then set a reminder to water your intentions and the plant. Make room for moments of pause between waterings to honor your intentions. Watch them physically grow and manifest.

Visualizing Your Sacred Workspace

Need some help visualizing and manifesting your sacred workspace? Create a digital vision board of your ideal space using Pinterest or another program. The images you pick can portray the aesthetic of your workspace but also how you want to feel in your workspace and the ideas you'd like it to foster. Set a reminder to refer back to this vision board to remind yourself of your vision.

You can also make a physical version of this board by printing out photos or artwork and attaching them to poster board. Place it in your workspace and refer to it often to remind yourself of your vision.

....

Thriving Affirmation

I am my own sacred space.

....

Chapter 9

A New Way to Work—
Pleasure, Joy, and Liberation

Kindness eases Change.
Love quiets fear.
And a sweet and powerful
Positive obsession
Blunts pain,
Diverts rage,
And engages each of us
In the greatest,
The most intense
Of our chosen struggles.
—Octavia E. Butler, *Parable of the Talents*

Janet Jackson released her *Control* album in 1986, the year I was born. The music video for the track "Pleasure Principle" was one of the first videos I remember watching, so thrilling in its simplicity, with Janet wearing a denim jacket over an all-black outfit while dancing in an empty warehouse. As simple as it was, something about her performance was magnetic. Only when I got much older did I understand why.

Control was her third studio album, and it contained many autobiographical themes related to major shifts that were occurring in her life at the time. She was a phoenix rising from the ashes of a huge transition. She had recently had her marriage to singer James DeBarge annulled, severed her business affairs from her father and manager Joseph and the rest of the Jackson family, and hired a new manager. Reflecting on that time, Janet remembers, "I just wanted to get out of the house, get out from under my father, which was one of the most difficult things that I had to do, telling him that I didn't want to work with him again." Janet Jackson transmuted her pain into power with this album and created a template and guidebook for Black female singers to follow for years to come.

Control is an album about a woman reclaiming her power from people who are undervaluing and managing her. It's a bold declaration of a woman who knows what she wants and is ready to make it plain. In "Pleasure Principle" she belts out lyrics such as "What I thought was happiness was only part-time bliss. You can take a bow."

Of course, Jackson's kick-ass song was building on the history and idea of the "pleasure principle," as coined by Sigmund Freud to describe the way that we seek out pleasure and avoid pain in order to satisfy our needs. In her 2019 book *The Pleasure Principle: Epicureanism: A Philosophy for Modern Living*, professor Catherine Wilson traced this idea back to the Epicurean movement, established by ancient

Greek philosopher Epicurus (341 BC–270 BC), Epicureans put pleasure at the center of living, believing that pleasure should be the basis of all our decisions. They taught that life should be free from anxiety and stress and we should bolster the importance of friendship and learning. They advocated living in the present moment without worry. There is a lot to learn from this philosophy—it seems to us not only liberating but actually radical. In a society that appears determined to keep us all perpetually overwhelmed, joy is a revolutionary act.

Pleasure holds a great deal of power and can be a pathway toward a more just and creative future. According to author and facilitator adrienne maree brown, "Pleasure activism is the work we do to reclaim our whole, happy, and satisfiable selves from the impacts, delusions, and limitations of oppression and/or supremacy. Pleasure activism asserts that we all need and deserve pleasure and that our social structures must reflect this. In this moment, we must prioritize the pleasure of those most impacted by oppression." Pleasure gives us courage to craft a new way of living and working with each other. As we work toward creating a more equitable and just economy and society, pleasure in the process is an ongoing reward, not something that we need to wait for, earn, or prove we are worthy to receive. We can enjoy the benefits of pleasure now.

As we have seen, emotional and spiritual reflection is a requirement for the grind culture detox process. We undergo this transformative process not because it is difficult and painful, but because we can use the experience to alchemize our pain and rise from its ashes. The grind culture detox leads us through shadow and struggle into another world and way of life.

Rewriting the Story of Self-Sacrifice

We can have a work life that's rooted in pleasure and joy and still make an impact. In order to do this, we have to unpack society's narrative that glorifies martyrdom. Consider the Christian narrative: in an act of redemptive suffering, we are told that Jesus died on the cross to pay for our sins, and that in order to be Christlike we must do the same by putting the needs and desires of others before ourselves in all circumstances, without questioning how this teaching perpetuates the toxic messaging of capitalism and patriarchy.

The allure of martyrdom keeps us chained to guilt and codependency. It keeps us striving for unattainable perfection. Reclaiming joy within the workplace will require us to relinquish martyrdom and step into our highest professional callings. After all, we can't reclaim pleasure and joy within our work life without unapologetically carving out space for ourselves to thrive.

Sometimes our highest calling might cause discomfort to others, but part of the future we are cocreating will consist of being able to assert our needs while simultaneously making space so that our needs don't overpower the ability of others to thrive. This can be tedious and delicate work. It requires a high level of self-knowledge, a commitment to inquiry over certainty, and the ability to build and sustain networks of community and relationship. It may be hard, but it's necessary and rewarding work. As speaker and author Glennon Doyle reminds us, "We can do hard things."

Remember, we live in a society that profits from perpetuating feelings of unworthiness and fear, because people are easier to control and their behavior is more predictable when they are disempowered. It's easier to shrink yourself into existing rules and norms when you feel unworthy or not enough. Grind culture keeps us on this hamster wheel of shame, guilt, and powerlessness, some of the lowest vibrational emotions that a human being can possess.

But another way is possible. This chapter will support your process of reclaiming joy within your workday so that you can access tools to thrive at any moment and build a practice of self-care, liberation, and pleasure that will sustain you forever.

The Emotional Guidance Scale

You have likely heard of the law of attraction, which asserts that when we feel good, we attract good things to us, because like attracts like. It seems simple enough—but when you are spiraling down a path of negative emotions caused by workplace stress and anxiety, it can feel difficult to reclaim yourself from negativity. Empty slogans like "Just think positive" or "Inhale the good and exhale the bullshit" simply don't cut it sometimes. What's worse, these slogans sometimes tempt us into bypassing difficult but necessary shadow work.

During these moments, you can use a tool called the Abraham-Hicks emotional guidance scale, which ranks the twenty-two most common human emotions by vibrational frequency.

Emotional Guidance Scale

1. Joy/Appreciation/Empowered/Freedom/Love

2. Passion

3. Enthusiasm/Eagerness/Happiness

4. Positive Expectation/Belief

5. Optimism

6. Hopefulness

7. Contentment

8. Boredom

9. Pessimism

10. Frustration/Irritation/Impatience

11. Overwhelm

12. Disappointment

13. Doubt

14. Worry

15. Blame

16. Discouragement

17. Anger

18. Revenge

19. Hatred/Rage

20. Jealousy

21. Insecurity/Guilt/Unworthiness

22. Fear/Grief/Depression/Despair/Powerlessness

On the following page is a visual representation of the general vibrational frequency of these emotions. Joy is one of the highest vibrational emotions you can have, the opposite and antidote to guilt and powerlessness. One thing I find fascinating about this spiral is that happiness is not the same as joy, nor does it vibrate at as high a frequency. There is so much in our culture oriented toward happiness as something we can buy, attain, or work toward. It becomes a shiny end product, the carrot on the stick that we will never quite be able to grab in grind culture. As we detox from grind culture, we set our sights higher than happiness. We look toward joy, toward liberation. These are not products but processes—we can find joy and liberation amid suffering and challenge. We can spread joy and liberation within our families and communities. Joy and liberation cannot

UPWARD SPIRAL

Joy
Freedom

Love
Empowerment

Passion
Eagerness

Enthusiasm
Happiness

Hopefulness
Optimism

Contentment
Belief

Positivity

BOREDOM

Frustration
Pessimism

Impatience
Irritation

Worry
Doubt

Rage
Anger

Jealousy
Hatred

Insecurity

Powerlessness
Guilt

DOWNWARD SPIRAL

be dangled in front of us, and they cannot be taken away. They are our birthright. I want you to imagine how your life might shift if you were able to reclaim joy within your workday. How might your overall perspective about your life and career shift if you were able to access joy as a regular emotion at work?

The Great Resignation and the Opportunity for More Joy at Work

The tide is turning. An increasing number of people are waking up to the fact that work doesn't have to be tedious and stress-inducing. At the time of this writing, we are experiencing what's being called the Great Resignation. As the COVID-19 pandemic continues to take lives and put vulnerable lives at risk, people are reevaluating what really matters to them. Many people learned that they could do their jobs just as effectively at home and have more freedom and autonomy and save time by not commuting to an office. Others are deciding that the jobs they had before the pandemic are not working for them anymore.

According to the US Labor Department, a record four million Americans resigned in April 2021 alone. People are reimagining what work-life balance means to them and many are choosing to quit as opposed to being demoralized at work for one moment longer. This mass resignation is forcing employers to reimagine alternatives to many of the restrictive policies that have caused people to walk. This includes rules related to dress code, time off and holidays, pay, and a deeper prioritizing of diversity, equity, and inclusion. These structural factors are critical to the conversation around what it means to enhance joy in the workplace.

For entrepreneurs who are running their own businesses or working as consultants outside of a nine-to-five, sometimes work-life boundaries get blurred. For these folks, increasing joy means becoming more vigilant about scheduling days off as well as time for wellness breaks in order to experience an overall greater sense of well-being and fulfillment.

As we explore some ways to infuse joy within your workday, we'll also walk through how to craft the personalized thriving tool kit that I've mentioned throughout this book. Your thriving tool kit is something you can always return to when you get caught up in grind culture again—as you inevitably will. Remember that healing isn't linear. The grind culture detox is about expansion through progress—not perfection.

Infusing Work with Joy

Nomakhosi Ndebele is a creative producer whose entrepreneurial drive has led her toward a multifaceted career as a heart-led brand strategist and style consultant. In this role, her passion and purpose come together to help spirited women reclaim their signature style by going beyond aesthetics for inner and outer transformation. She works with her clients on embodying joy and pleasure through fashion. For Nomakhosi, fashion is more than clothing; it represents a lifestyle, a way of connecting to a person's inner essence. She has decided to live life on her own terms and outside of society's limited expectations. "You're going to make decisions in life that people around you who are living on that level of limitation. . . they're going to look at you and question everything that you do, and you have to be okay with that. You have to have that courage and conviction. It has to be something within you that you just know. There's another way to live life beyond what I've been taught and sold. That was somebody else's dream. That's not my dream."

To support her journey and balance the courage and difficulty of making her own way, Nomakhosi organizes her days around joy and pleasure. Here are some of her daily practices:

> *Get into a positive flow state first thing in the morning.* Start your day with the work that excites you; this sets the tone for the rest of your day. Even if you're working for somebody else, do the enjoyable tasks first.

> *Infuse play into your work.* Make things a game; challenge yourself to do sprints of work with rest in between. Dance or listen to music while you work. Laugh with your clients.

> *Get dressed and ready for work with intention and joy.* Make it fun by thinking about what you want for your day, how you will surprise and delight yourself with your self-expression. Ask yourself, *What do I want to express through my outfit or my look?*

Set intentions for the day. If you have a meeting or appointments, decide how you're going to show up for these activities. What is your highest purpose, even within the boring tasks?

Find your originality. Even people whose job requires a uniform have ways to enhance their essence— how you style your hair, your makeup, etc. For example, if you're a nurse and you have to wear scrubs, you could get your scrubs tailored. You don't have to necessarily wear baggy scrubs. You can play with your uniform in an appropriate, professional way. It's so important to feel confident in how you look and really be able to express your inner essence through your outer expression.

Mirror Magic Exercise

Here's a practice that Nomakhosi does on a daily basis in order to reprogram her subconscious mind to cultivate more joy in her work life, facilitate healing, set intentions and affirmations, and build in time for self-reflection. When done in a safe and sacred way, looking in the mirror can be a powerful transformational tool.

To start, set the scene. Use a mirror you really like— whatever you have access to that has good energy. Allow yourself to get really calm and relaxed so that you can hack your subconscious. You may want to set the mood with soothing music or candlelight. Plan for between ten and twenty minutes of uninterrupted time to start. To begin the ritual, take a few deep breaths and look deep into your own eyes.

As you gaze into your eyes, repeat affirmations that celebrate you and affirm who you are in this moment. Repeat, "I am proud of _____" and follow that with a few things that you are proud of yourself for. Next, affirm self-love by saying, "I love you, _____" and your name. Let whatever emotions come up flow without judgment, staying vulnerable and accepting the love you are giving yourself. Next, repeat any affirmations you are working with in the current moment, perhaps one from the chapters in this book. Repeat these for five minutes in the mirror on a daily basis.

Follow those five minutes or more with statements of what you want to embody. If it's abundance, for example, repeat in the mirror, "I am abundant. I am worthy of abundance. I am worthy of luxury. I am worthy of ease." Do this for another five minutes. With your words, invite whatever quality you are cultivating to make a home in your physical body, in the deep pools of your eyes, in your beating heart.

Take a moment to meditate or journal about the experience before closing out this ritual. Remember, you can safely sit in any emotion that comes up for you in this time.

Your Thriving Tool Kit

Your ongoing journey toward work-life liberation is just beginning. It will be long and winding, with successes and setbacks, but it will always be a process. In light of this, I invite you to pack a thriving tool kit. This is a collection of exercises, affirmations, mental models, strategies, and healing modalities to which you can return for inspiration, rejuvenation, and stamina to stay the course as you do the work of divesting and healing from grind culture.

The average adult in the United States will spend most of their waking hours at work. Doesn't it make sense for us to regularly access joy and pleasure at work so that we can reclaim our power, maintain our humanity, and fulfill our deepest purpose? Life can get stressful, busy, and chaotic. Even if we have a series of good days, grind culture can pull us back into its rut. We can forget to pour into ourselves as much as we pour into others. We can lose track of boundaries and self-care. We might ease up on our commitment to get into nature or to rest and sleep. In these moments, there's no need for judgment or shame. We all fall back into toxic cycles. Remember, this is a process. Perfection is a grind culture myth.

In fact, falling back into our old patterns can often provide a beautiful learning opportunity. When we realize that we're back in the cycle of grind culture, we know that we have built up awareness practices and that we are learning to trust and rely on ourselves to take care of ourselves and our work in a different way. In those moments, we can refer back to our thriving tool kit to reclaim joy within our workday.

I encourage you to read through the following exercise, and then write down your thriving tool kit in your journal or type it up and print it out to put it somewhere you'll see it every day. You can also create thriving tool kit reminders and use it as a diagnostic tool throughout your week or month. I also encourage you to return to the tool kit on a regular basis, perhaps with the changes of the seasons, and swap out activities and update things as you go. This is a living document of an ongoing process to cultivate joy and liberation in your work and life.

Choose Your Thriving Activities

First, take some time to write down five activities from each of the following categories. Keep these activities doable and diverse in terms of intensity and amount of time required. Avoid including anything that makes you feel guilty or like you "should" do it. Bring on things that feel joyful, possible, and freeing.

> *Movement.* Examples: practice yoga, take a walk around the neighborhood, go to the gym, go hiking, do fifty jumping jacks, dance with the kids, stretch for fifteen minutes, try a new movement class, schedule a game or match with a friend.

Nutrition. Examples: make a smoothie, take a multivitamin, make a cup of herbal tea, eat more fresh fruits and vegetables, drink a glass of water, try a new recipe, cook a vegan meal.

Creativity. Examples: paint, color in a coloring book, take photos on a nature walk, listen to your favorite album without skipping songs, play an instrument or sing, write a haiku, take a class that sparks your creativity, craft, read a novel, freewrite for fifteen minutes.

Mindfulness. Examples: meditate for fifteen minutes, listen to a sound healing, listen to binaural beats, take a forest bath, journal, meditate with a favorite crystal, do a body scan, practice grounding by going barefoot in nature.

Learning. Examples: take a course or attend a workshop, read a nonfiction book, listen to a podcast, ask an elder to tell you a story, enlist a librarian to help you find a great book you wouldn't otherwise know about, gather and process historical research on a current social problem, ask a friend to explain more about a topic they really love or nerd out about.

Rest. Examples: have a phone-free hour, do a social media–free day, have an audio-only meeting day, visit a sensory deprivation tank, take a forest bath, sleep with an eye mask, attend a silent retreat, listen to a self-hypnosis script, take a nap, go to bed early.

Social connection. Examples: take a hike with family or friends, engage in a family reading night, go to your local farmers market, catch up with a friend or family member, attend a retreat, host a potluck or picnic.

Now that you have at least thirty-five potential activities in your thriving tool kit, start by choosing three from three different categories and take a moment to schedule them in your calendar within a given week. Pay attention to picking activities from multiple categories in order to ensure you are getting a balance of restoration and regeneration. If three restorative activities seems easy to achieve, then challenge yourself to schedule four or five restorative activities per week in your calendar. Make sure to start where you are and approach this activity from a place of curiosity and desire for improvement.

Crafting a Joyous Workflow (Your Joy Checklist)

Once you've had a chance to implement some changes in your routine and distance yourself from grind culture, take a moment to check in with yourself to see how it's all going. Assessing your progress along the grind culture detox path isn't meant to identify points of success or failure; rather, it's an opportunity to see what's working and what isn't, and where you have room to make more positive change. Feel free to check in with yourself daily, weekly, monthly, or quarterly, as your schedule allows and as you feel compelled to.

- How does my workspace feed my five senses (or not)?

- Am I starting my days with my morning ritual?

- Is there space in my calendar for my physical needs, such as meal and bathroom breaks, breastfeeding, showering and getting dressed, and stretching?

- Is there space in my calendar for my emotional needs, such as time to decompress after meetings and time for reflection?

- Is there space in my calendar for my spiritual needs, such as meditation, tarot, prayer, yoga, or somatics?

- Is there an opportunity to cultivate time spent outdoors today?

- How's my water intake?

- Have I been taking my thriving supplements?

- How can I infuse one of my creative passions into each day's workflow?

- Have I had a chance to do neck and shoulder stretches daily?

- Have I made space for gratitude daily?

Workplace Joy Bingo

Try using the template on the following page to make your own Workplace Joy Bingo. Add any small, doable activities you want, and see if you can get a string of four or five in a row as you do the activities throughout your day.

....

Thriving Affirmation

Joy is a pleasurable and a revolutionary act.

....

Workspace Joy Bingo

Thriving with Heather

2 min dance party to your favorite song	Light your favorite incense	Make a cup of tea	Take your vitamins	Do a 5 min yoga sequence on Pintrest
Do a task while listening to your favorite podcast	Take a 10 minute walk around your neighborhood	Eat a healthy snack	Drink a glass of water	Hold onto your favorite crystal
Take a salt bath while checking emails	Take 3 deep breaths	Inhale your favorite aromatherapy spray	Use a CBD vape pen for anxiety	Water your plants
Affirm 3 things you're grateful for	Set an intention for the future	Use a pen with your favorite colored ink.	Light some palo santo	Roll your neck and shoulders
Look into a kaliedoscope or something else that sparks imagination	Blow bubbles at your desk	Jump rope 100 times	Do a downward dog	Meditate for 5 minutes
Read your favorite motivational quote	Watch a naturescape on YouTube	Take a short nap	Sit on a beanbag chair	Stand on a reflexology mat

Afterword

We hold this myth to be potential
Not self evident alone but equational;
Another Dimension
Of another kind of Living Life
—Sun Ra, "We Hold This Myth To Be Potential"

In 2014, I worked abroad as a teacher for a company that trained business professionals in advanced English. I was living my bohemian dream, traveling around the world, having my own *Eat, Pray, Love* experience. I had spent the previous six months in northern Thailand in a town called Lampang and was now getting a taste of the Turkish experience in Istanbul. While there, I learned a great deal about the meaning of leisure and had time to practice the art of slowing down. Everything in the city seemed to be asking me to relinquish my quick and easy habits and replace them with slow and steady ones.

One of my favorite parts about Turkish culture is that there is always time for tea. No matter where you go—whether it's a school, a mosque, or a cell phone store—you will be offered tea—an invitation to pause and enjoy a sacred moment of life.

By the time I was in my sixth month in Turkey, I had leaned into life at a slower pace and was enjoying several cups of tea a day as well as a deeper appreciation for the little things like fresh baked bread and Turkish delight.

However, I was also feeling restless, and I was ready to go back home to California. I was ready to go back to a place where people shared common experiences with me. I was feeling nostalgic and homesick for the good the United States had to offer. I missed the culture, and the Black culture in America in particular. I missed being able to wear my hair in an afro and not get gawked at or treated like I was an alien. I missed being able to read a menu and understand it. I missed connecting with folks who liked similar music. I missed the beautiful coastline along Highway 1. I missed my family. I was ready to go home. I was also ready to go back and implement some of the learnings that I had encountered during my travels abroad.

One night, I was hanging out at a hostel called the Magic Bus near Taksim Street in Istanbul, an eclectic haven of hippies, bohemians, and backpackers visiting from all over the world. Never had I been surrounded by such a diverse group of people. It was quite a treat. On this particular evening, I was sitting with travelers from South Africa, Syria, Iraq, Peru, Spain, the United States, Ukraine, Russia, Turkey, and Mali. We talked all night, connecting over ideas, discussing politics, and just laughing and holding space for each other. That night I let the group know that I thought it might be time to move back home. The group was shocked. Each person tried to convince me to stay abroad. Anywhere but the United States, or "the belly of the beast," as one person said.

As the conversation progressed, I started to feel offended and indignant. How dare they talk about my home like this? Yes, parts of it sucked, but what did they know? My relationship to US citizenship had changed while I was living abroad. I became oddly patriotic, an attitude I never held on to before my time away.

And yet, when I moved back, I *did* see my world differently. Aspects of society that I had accepted as "just the way things are" no longer sat well with me. The conversation around police brutality was continuing to grow at that time, and the Black Lives Matter movement was flourishing. While I'd been abroad, I'd been hit very hard by the murder of Trayvon Martin, an unarmed African American teenager who was shot at his father's townhome complex, and I found myself getting into racial debates with white males abroad who defended Martin's shooting. It was maddening and isolating. When I came home, however, I got even more scared and infuriated by the total lack of conversation and the silence around these issues in professional spaces.

When I came back, I was an English as a Second Language teacher in San Francisco. I was the only Black woman on staff. Very often, when police shootings were in the news, no one at work would talk about it. There was no place to process these tragic events. It felt so isolating to pretend that these things weren't happening.

These moments radicalized me. When I reflect back on that spring evening at the Magic Bus hostel, I do empathize with the sentiments of my international friends. In some ways, the United States *is* the belly of the beast—a place where the dollar is paramount, where work is virtuous, and more work is most important thing we can do. It's where our value is our output, end of story. I see things differently now.

It's been a challenge to bring home the consciousness of leisure that I had while living abroad. Our society isn't built for tea breaks, long walks, family meals, vacations, restful mornings, and late-night conversations with friends. But I continue to carry a golden objective: I will claim and hold on to that liberatory sense of leisure by any means necessary. I will never again work without that objective in mind. For me, it's a matter of survival. I slow down and rest for my ancestors who couldn't. I rest for my child and the generations who will care for this earth long after I am gone. Resting is a deeply political act.

I have no regrets about choosing the United States as my home, despite the abusive and traumatic events that my ancestors experienced. This is the place where I am answering the call of becoming a conscious cocreator of the society I want for future generations, knowing it starts with me but doesn't end with me. As I work to cocreate this new world, I will not be swayed by fear or anxiety. I am activated instead by reverence for my ancestors who were displaced, killed, and enslaved in the name of building this country. I hold the vision of my ancestors as I work to cocreate an American dream rooted in equity and sovereignty.

As stated in the Declaration of Independence,

> Whenever any Form of Government becomes destructive of these ends, it is the Right of the People to alter or to abolish it, and to institute new Government, laying its foundation on such principles and organizing its powers in such form, as to them shall seem most likely to effect their Safety and Happiness.

It is time to rewrite the rules and cocreate a world outside of grind culture.

My hope is that this book acts not only as a guide to help you liberate and empower yourself toward a work life that is filled with authentic joy, personal fulfillment, and times of restorative rest, but also as a call to action. Now more than ever, we need to instill within our personal spaces and our communities the values and practices that stand in opposition to grind culture. In embracing and owning your own right to rest, heal, and thrive, I invite you to encourage others in your social circle and wider communities to do so as well. Consider starting a group with like-minded friends where you can share your experiences as you work through recognizing and rejecting the insidious cultural attitudes of grind culture. Reach out and ask questions, of yourself and others. Create sacred space, rest without shame or guilt, and remind yourself and others often that you are worthy of a world in which your value arises from the mere fact of your existence, not what you produce.

As we boldly embrace the unknown, we will need to cultivate futurist visioning. Futurist visioning helps us to plan and prepare for a world beyond our wildest dreams. It honors the unknown itself as a generative space. It asks us to embrace inquiry over certainty, process over product, leaning into questions like, "How might we?" rather than "How will we?" Futurist visioning invites us to dwell in the possibility of collective liberation. We've witnessed oppressive systems thrive and adapt throughout the centuries to the detriment of the earth and humanity. We know that old ways of thinking and acting no longer serve our collective story. As we face enormous challenges and terrifying outcomes, our imagination may be the thing that saves us.

Afrofuturism is an aesthetic, a philosophy, and a literary genre that combines a variety of cultural mediums, including science fiction, African cosmology, historical fiction, and fantasy to examine and critique the current realities of Black experiences while reinventing new possibilities. Afrofuturist author Ytasha Womack describes it as "a way of bridging the future and the past and essentially helping to reimagine the experience of people of color." Afrofuturism has everything to do with being dissatisfied with the current reality of an oppressed existence, so much so that authors, thinkers, and theologians create a new hypothetical world. It's distinct from many science fiction or techno-futurist impulses, however, because it holds an intrinsic awareness and reverence for the past that's anchored by a deep need to transcend it.

Now more than ever, people all over the world are uncovering hidden stories, rejecting white supremacist narratives, and using nuggets of truth found in the vaults of the collective histories of our ancestors. Examples include everything from television shows like *Watchmen* and *Lovecraft Country* to the novels of Octavia E. Butler and N. K. Jemisin, museum shows, dance and theater pieces, and the aesthetics of Black artists like Missy Elliott and Janelle Monáe. Through an Afrofuturist approach, we're reaching for alternative realities in which we define ourselves for ourselves rather than relying on an oppressive system to define us. Because the present looks grim, we need hope and creativity. Afrofuturism can inspire in all of us the energy, boldness, and vision we need to cocreate our individual and collective futures.

When we divest from grind culture, we invest in cultivating work-life liberation through more creation and less production. We weave the fabric of a society that prioritizes a culture of well-being by promoting more intersectional wellness in our personal and professional lives. I don't know about you, but I was put on this earth to do more than produce; I'm here to create. Creation is the vision, the goal, and the process. I am worth more than what I can produce, and I choose life.

Acknowledgments

Gratitude is a powerful medicine, and I would like to extend it to the following:

To my mother for instilling me with a solid foundation of spirituality and holistic medicine and lighting within me a passion for healing and well-being.

To my husband and life partner Kevin, for supporting me and elevating me during the euphoric and challenging moments of writing this book.

To Makiah Lewis, Monique Melton, Nakia Dillard, Cameo Turner, Emilyn Sosa, and Nomakhosi Ndebele who shared their inspiring stories and healing wisdom to bring these ideas to life.

To the Hierophant Publishing team for the love and care you provided to bring this vision to life.

Last and certainly not least, my deepest gratitude for my ancestors and the land of Turtle Island who carried me through this process.

I am because we are.

About the Author

Heather Archer is a certified life coach with specialties in sound healing, Reiki yoga, and hypnotherapy. Her life's mission is to live a liberated work-life while helping her community to thrive in their personal and professional lives. She does this through hosting workshops, retreats, and nature-based events that center healing and wellness for stressed-out professionals.

With an educational background from Smith College and New York University and over fifteen years of experience with teacher training and curriculum development, Heather weaves her academic and organizational background with her work as a workplace wellness coach and healer to create a transformational learning experience for you on your transformative journey from surviving to thriving.

You can learn more about her work at www.thrivingwithheather.com.

Hier◯phant publishing

books that inspire your body, mind, and spirit

San Antonio, TX
www.hierophantpublishing.com